DENIS H. STOTT, Ph.D., is an emeritus psychology professor and the author of seven books in the fields of delinquency and behavior problems.

HELPING THE MALADJUSTED CHILD

A Guide for Parents and Teachers

Denis H. Stott

A SPECTRUM BOOK

Prentice-Hall, Inc., Englewood Cliffs, New Jersey 07632

Library of Congress Cataloging in Publication Data

Stott, D. H. (Denis Herbert), 1909-
    Helping the maladjusted child.

    "A Spectrum Book."
    Bibliography: p.
    Includes index.
    1. Child psychopathology.   2. Parental depriva-
tion.   3. Child psychotherapy.   4. Psychiatric social
work.   I. Title.
RJ499.S7977 1982   618.92'89   82-11217

ISBN 0-13-387068-5

ISBN 0-13-387050-2 (PBK.)

This Spectrum Book is available to businesses and organizations at a
special discount when ordered in large quantities. For
information, contact Prentice-Hall, Inc., General Publishing
Division, Special Sales, Englewood Cliffs, N.J. 07632.

Printed in the United States of America

10   9   8   7   6   5   4   3   2   1

Editorial/production supervision: Inkwell
Manufacturing buyer: Cathie Lenard

Prentice-Hall International, Inc., *London*
Prentice-Hall of Australia Pty. Limited, *Sydney*
Prentice-Hall of Canada, Inc., *Toronto*
Prentice-Hall of India Private Limited, *New Delhi*
Prentice-Hall of Japan, Inc., *Tokyo*
Prentice-Hall of Southeast Asia Pte. Ltd., *Singapore*
Whitehall Books Limited, Wellington, *New Zealand*

Contents

Preface

This book has been written for:

- Those whose work brings them into contact with maladjusted or deviant young people, and who seek ways of understanding and helping them.
- Parents whose children have been giving them cause for concern or who are going through a difficult period.
- Students who aim to qualify themselves in the professions with the responsibility of counselling young people and their parents.

For all these people:

- This book first clears up what is maladjusted, and what is only rebellious or unusual behavior.
- It describes the types of maladjustment and how they can be recognized.
- It discusses what makes children maladjusted, particularly the sorts of family stresses that deprive children of their confidence in the adult world.

- Finally, it offers counsel about how to help each type of maladjusted child settle down as a useful and happy citizen.

The contents of the book are summarized chapter by chapter as follows:

- *Chapter One* defines maladjustment and distinguishes it from other kinds of unusual or undesirable behavior. Some children are situation-valuable, and hence appear, in interviews, in court, and in other places of authority as misleadingly normal. For effective treatment, the nature and causes of the various types of behavior disturbance need to be understood.
- *Chapter Two* reviews the issues of the child's separation from the mother and deprivation of mother-love. Their effects are not as clear cut or as alarming, as earlier studies suggested. Nevertheless, it is recognized that for healthy emotional development, a child needs a permanent and secure attachment to a loving adult.
- *Chapter Three* describes the child's reactions to deprivation. The most common reactions are Hostility, which arises from a fear of rejection or abandonment by the loved adult; and abnormal behavior in the form of thoughtless excitement seeking and other forms of compulsive avoidance in order to block the pain of deprivation.
- *Chapter Four* suggests measures for alleviating the plight of the deprived child, especially by working with the parents to remove the source of the deprivation. The child may temporarily have to be taken into residential care, the form and aims of which are discussed
- *Chapter Five* pinpoints the types of family situations which may deprive the child of a sense of being cherished by loyal and loving parents. These maladjustment producing situations are divided into four main groups, and typical defects in parent-child relationships are described as a guide to the understanding of the child's emotional disturbance.
- *Chapter Six* outlines ways in which parents and teachers can help children who are hostile or dominated by avoidance compulsions.
- *Chapter Seven* deals with two typical handicaps of temperament. These are Unforthcomingness (a fear of facing the challenges of life and of learning), and Overdependence. Both can lead to a retreat into retardation. Measures are proposed for encouraging children suffering from these handicaps to take their part in life along with other children.
- *Chapter Eight* discusses Inconsequence ("Hyperactivity") and indifference to affection as two further handicaps of temperament. It is crucial to distinguish between the hyperactive child who wants to "push the world around" and the type who suffers from neuro-

logical dysfunction. Treatment of the hyperactive child consists in training the youngster to control his or her own behavior. Drugs hinder this process. Where the child cannot achieve behavioral control, he or she should be medically examined for oxygen deprivation, metabolic disturbances, and food allergies.

- *Chapter Nine* outlines a program for long term prevention of maladjustment, drawing on recent findings relating prenatal damage to the mother's unhappiness during pregnancy. Building stable communities provides safeguards against both constitutional vulnerability to behavior problems and deprivation. Family stability depends upon a tradition of restraint rather than giving way to free expression of anger.

HELPING THE MALADJUSTED CHILD

chapter one

Recognizing and understanding maladjustment

WHAT IS NOT MALADJUSTED

"There's nowt so queer as fowks," runs an old proverb from Yorkshire, England. We never cease to be surprised at the strange ways of our friends and acquaintances. Nevertheless the great majority of folks get along in their own way, without doing much harm to themselves or to other people. They choose forms of adjustment to life that may strike other people as queer. Yet—unless we ourselves have lost our sense of proportion—we do not regard the whole world as mad or maladjusted. By some unconscious yardstick we are able to distinguish this almost universal queerness—or, to be more objective, variability—in our fellow beings from psychosis, neurosis, or, in the case of children, maladjustment.

Since this book is about maladjustment, we have first to clarify this distinction between maladjustment and the many variants of normality. Obviously maladjustment is not just troublesome or disapproved behavior. Children with very dominant personalities may use all sorts of strategies to get their way. Some fly into tempers, whine, or develop feeding or bowel problems to control their parents. Others feign helplessness or even retardation as a means of establishing a sort of master- or mistress-servant relationship with their parents—with themselves as the masters or mistresses. We may call this "strategic troublesomeness."

Such attempts by children to get their own way—a normal human characteristic—can be reinforced when parents give in to them. An essentially stable child then becomes what disapproving relatives and friends describe as "an unholy terror." Drillien,[1] in her well-known follow-up study of children from birth, was surprised to find how many who were troublesome at home showed no signs whatsoever of behavioral disturbance in school. I remember a little girl who was positively timid and meek in school but who controlled her mother by continual temper tantrums.

The same can be said of other behavior of which adults disapprove. Following their cultural tradition and class-consciousness, parents usually have pretty definite ideas about which careers they don't wish their children to follow. Yet the history of art, literature, and invention is full of instances of sons' and daughters' realizing their creativity in the face of parental opposition. Clothing and speech have always been so highly regarded as the identification marks of tribe or social class that community elders are apt to take exception to deviant forms of dress or speech in the young. Young people who deviate in these respects are not for that reason maladjusted. They may only be trying to assert their independence or to conform to the ways of a peer group that is challenging some of the conventions of the older generation. Some young people develop special interests that neither their parents nor their peers understand, and, rather than renouncing these interests, they become loners.

Others are blessed, or cursed, with what is regarded as an excessive need for personal independence; they seem to have a constitutional disinclination, or inability, to conform. These individualists may take pride in doing things differently, or they may insist in trying to think out solutions themselves rather than adopting the solutions of others. Often the solutions of these "young geniuses" don't work out because of their lack of knowledge and experience, and they would do better for themselves in a conventional sense if only they would be good little students who learn the art of passing examinations by reproducing the information and the ideas they have been taught. As for their careers, creativity is in fact more often a drawback than an asset, because only the lucky few gain recognition. Nevertheless, we cannot say that creativity is a form of maladjustment as we conceive the term, even though creative persons usually fail to adapt themselves to the accepted values of their society and age. It's just that their goals are different.

There is also considerable uncertainty about the symptoms of maladjustment. Parents may become less anxious if they know that many of its supposed signs are too widespread among children in general to have much significance. In an American study,[2] in which a random cross-section of mothers were interviewed, it was found that, among their children aged six to twelve years, no less than 43 percent had seven or more specific fears or worries. In the same group, 28 percent lost their tempers twice a week or more. In fact, my own casework experience has shown that being "too good" as a young child was more often associated with later trouble than normal naughtiness. And this finding certainly applies, for example, to the growing boy who is always willing and eager to do household jobs, compared with the one who grumbles and tries to get out of them if he can.

WHAT IS MALADJUSTMENT?

So much for what maladjustment is not. We need a statement of what it is. Mary Cleugh[3] has proposed the following as a definition: Children may be considered maladjusted if their behavior, if they persist in it, is likely to render them unfit to play their part and to hold their own in society. The criterion for maladjustment that I have often used is whether the child acts against his or her own best interests (with "best" implying the child's interests over the long term). Persons who persistently yield to impulses that afford them immediate gratification but that later involve them in trouble would by this definition be considered "maladjusted."

Both these definitions imply an inability or refusal to learn from the consequences of behaving in a certain way. The touchstone of maladjustment is that normal discipline, which the majority of children heed, is ineffective; the maladjusted child is undeterrable. This characteristic, as we shall see in the discussion on the handling of maladjusted children, has important implications for the use of punishment in the home and the school. Mary Cleugh follows up her definition by emphasizing, as I have done, that, just because behavior is inconvenient or troublesome to an adult, it is not for that reason alone maladjusted. But since troublesome, antisocial children antagonize people and invite rejection, they deprive themselves of a basic need for adult affection and care. In doing so they act against their own best interests and must therefore be rated as maladjusted. To use a well-known phrase, such children, by continually creating more difficult situations for themselves, become their own worst enemies.

ONLY BEHAVIOR, NOT THOUGHTS OR FEELINGS, CAN BE CALLED MALADJUSTED

Our concept of maladjustment has to be further clarified. For one thing, maladjustment is a matter of behavior. It is not what we think or feel but what we do that makes us maladjusted. The thoughts that enter our minds, and the feelings that well up in us are primitive, instinctive reactions. These "promptings to action" have had value in human evolution and they still have value now. At a very early stage, mechanisms were developed to control primitive instinctive responses. We have all experienced nearly irresistible impulses to act in ways that would harm us. Yet we are usually able to hold ourselves back. It is as if we are able to rehearse the action in our minds and see its consequences. Failure to carry out such mental rehearsals is a major cause of maladjustment. It is not accurate to say that we cannot control our feelings and thoughts, for we have the capacity to dismiss feelings and thoughts which could have dangerous consequences. It is even possible to exercise this internal censorship before we are consciously aware of the dangerous impulse.

The German poet Schiller maintained that the highest level of moral development was the ability to train oneself not to think unworthy thoughts. It is doubtful whether he ever reached this level of saintliness. If he did it was by dismissing these thoughts so rapidly that he was hardly aware of them. Schiller was correct in the sense that the more we allow ourselves to dwell upon our frustrations and antagonisms, the more difficult it is to avoid reacting unwisely to them. How we are able to deal with them without "jumping out of the frying pan and into the fire" is, however, one of the aspects of our behavioral system to be discussed. At this point we can say that censoring or avoiding potentially dangerous impulses is vital to our nature, since human society would be impossible if we didn't. The popular idea that strong feelings which are "bottled up" can be harmful is an example of primitive reasoning by material analogies. The effects of pressure inside a bottle cannot be compared to the pressure we feel to act. People who feel that they have to express their anger are more likely to do themselves harm than people who are able to contain their feelings. The same can be said of feelings of anxiety, which arise when we don't feel confident in dealing with a threat or achieving a goal. Continued severe anxiety may get the better of a person and induce a desperate, ill-considered action which is against that person's interests; but it is the action and not the anxiety which ranks as maladjusted.

UNWILLED BEHAVIOR

The second limitation to our concept is that maladjustment applies only to behavior designed to have some effect. This definition excludes autism, which is now regarded as a severe learning disorder, and, what are broadly termed, habit disorders. Some of these disorders—twitches and other involuntary movements and exaggerated startle reactions—are indications of localized neural dysfunction, and they can occur in anyone during periods of fatigue. Others are disturbances of bodily function; the most common are bedwetting and asthma. Both of these habit disorders can be brought on by stress, but they can also occur without any provocation and apart from significant behavior disturbance. There is probably too great a readiness at the present time to see them as symptoms of emotional upset. In any case, it is misleading to rate them as indications of maladjustment.

A third class of habit disorders may be described as "bad personal habits," (in the old-fashioned sense). The most common is nailbiting—statistically associated with maladjustment only after the age of nine years. More alarming types of this disorder are forms of self-mutilation: pulling out hair, and weird limb movements.

All these habit disorders share a common feature: they are not directed to achieving change in the outside world. In maladjusted behavior, on the other hand, there seems to be a goal: children aim at creating or maintaining a relationship with other people and/or their surroundings which is detrimental to their interests. It is these forms of behavior disturbance which are the subject of this book.

MALADJUSTMENT IS NOT MANIFEST
AT ALL TIMES

There are two main reasons why many maladjusted children go unde-
tected. The first is a misconception which causes confusion—and sometimes mistreatment or ill treatment—in several areas of handicap. Once a
child is placed in an accepted official category—"labeled" as retarded,
perceptually handicapped, learning disabled, maladjusted, and so on—
people view that child as different in some mysterious way. I recall inviting
a young professional in the field of retardation to speak to my students
about the excellent work he was doing in guiding mentally handicapped
adults towards normality. He described a young woman who looked,
spoke, and acted completely normal—"so that you wouldn't know she was
retarded." The label had outlived reality.

In the same way, people use the term "maladjustment" as a self-
explanatory label and expect maladjusted children to constantly exhibit
their disturbance. If such children—so far as can be seen—are behaving
normally, those making judgment find it hard to believe that they are
maladjusted. Many children who have maladjusted phases or outbreaks
behave normally for the greater part of the time. Only when they find
themselves in a situation which triggers their vulnerability—or when their
resources are drained by physical stress—do they revert to the maladaptive
behavior pattern.

Children whose confidence in the loyalty of their parents—or whoever they look to for support and affection—has been undermined, are
prone to phases of moody hostility. If they are corrected or punished,
they feel rejected and react defiantly, as if they want to get rejection in
first; but when they feel accepted, their anxiety for affection may make
them over-good and over-helpful children. Many delinquent youths I have
known would do the housework for their mothers, mind the baby for her,
and buy her expensive presents—all from the fear of losing her. But when
some incident occurred which reminded them of their mother's unreliability, they would steal from her or run away from home and commit
thefts. On encountering some reminder of a distressing family situation, a
child may resort to "mad" behavior: running out of the school for no
apparent reason, attacking other children or the teacher, stealing impul-
sively, or seeking excitement by foolish or hazardous escapades. When
such children are absorbed in some fulfilling activity and can forget their
anxieties, they will be rational, stable, and more interested in school.

The maladjustment of some children is due to their inability to inhibit impulses to do foolish or dangerous things. In their normal state they appear likeable, hardworking, intelligent, and stable. But then some mischievous or delinquent peer challenges them to commit a foolhardy prank or to join in a delinquent adventure, and, without a second thought, they are into trouble.

All these children are *situation-vulnerable,* and their maladjustment consists of *situation-attitudes* which remain hidden until they find themselves in the particular situation that touches off their weakness. Their vulnerability can be heightened by the shock of an injury (especially to the head, hands, or feet) or by involvement in a frightening episode—an explosion, for example. I know of several instances in which stable, sensible, dutiful children have plunged into a phase of uncontrolled delinquency following such an accident or shock.

Because these situation-vulnerable children are so deceptively normal most of the time, their outbreaks are interpreted as sheer willfulness, naughtiness, or lack of discipline—and the child is punished accordingly. During my stay in Glasgow—from the mid-1950's to the mid-1960's—certain pupils were beaten with a strap two or three times a day by different teachers during phases of disturbed behavior; naturally, if they were prone to hostility, this sort of aggression confirmed their hostility and provoked them to even greater retaliation.

Emotionally vulnerable children seldom display their maladaptive behavior in front of people in an official position—probation officers, judges, for example. A probation office or a courtroom is not the kind of environment that touches them off or gives them an opportunity for deviant behavior. Consequently, many probation officers allow themselves to be convinced by theoretical sociologists that their clients are ordinary, well-adjusted, young people acting in accordance with an accepted pattern of behavior (The fact is that only a minority of even the most underprivileged children become serious delinquents). Likewise, many judges, who only see the young offender on his or her best behavior in a courtroom, insist that few delinquents are maladjusted. Not even a psychiatrist can be sure of spotting proneness to maladjustment in an interview. John Bowlby, a highly regarded psychiatrist, estimated that he would not be able to detect more than half the cases in this way. On the other hand, parents or teachers, who see children for a major part of their waking life, are in a position to observe the maladjusted behavior, even though it may occur only occasionally. It follows that officials who see these children for a short time—under conditions of formality when the youngster is probably overawed—should obtain systematic reports from parents and teachers about everday behavior patterns.

It should be mentioned, in order to forestall misunderstanding, that some kinds of maladjustment are likely to be in evidence all the time: the moodiness and mute antagonism of severe hostility, a constitutional lack of confidence, and the sorts of depression which arise from chronic illness, lack of sleep, or continuous exposure to stressful conditions.

MALADJUSTMENT AND DISCIPLINE

There is another powerful reason why so many of those who have to deal with children who persistently misbehave are unwilling to accept the possibility that they may be maladjusted: the only justification for punishment is that these children will heed it and mend their ways. I have mentioned that an inability to do so may be the first major signal of maladjustment. If certain children are unable to control their behavior—as the concept of maladjustment implies—it amounts to insensitivity or even cruelty to go on punishing them. Yet teachers and judges are only too aware that without the deterrence of punishment, ordinary people, young or old, will take advantage of the situation. The lootings which have occurred in times of electricity failure or the disregard for traffic regulations—when the chances of being caught are small or the penalities light—reveal the need for a system of law and its efficient enforcement. But any system of deterrence has to be justified by the moral principle that people are responsible for their actions. From the age of a year or so, a child is implicitly held responsible for behavior he or she can control. Human beings do not have built-in, instinctive mechanisms for observing social discipline, as ants and bees have. Consequently, all traditional human groups have imposed a system of discipline on their members, and the principle of personal responsibility has to be maintained as the foundation for a code of behavior and its enforcement.

The socially enforced code of behavior becomes an important determinant of each individual's actions. People of normal motivation weigh the consequences of obeying or disobeying the code according to how they conceive their personal goals. A prerequisite for doing this is the person's ability to consider consequences and to control his or her own behavior.

The maladjusted person, adult or child, is unable to do this. So, the enforcement of a code has the practical effect of identifying the maladjusted. For them, the further imposition of disciplinary measures serves no useful purpose. It is at this point—when the child's inability to respond to discipline is apparent—that the reasons for the disturbed behavior have to be investigated. It is not contradictory to insist upon the enforcement of a code of discipline that places limits on the assertiveness or natural selfishness of the normal majority while providing more appropriate treatment and care for the maladjusted.

MALADJUSTMENT IS NOT A MERE CULTURAL ARTIFACT

Disturbed behavior in disadvantaged localities—where the incidence of both delinquency and maladjustment is high—is sometimes viewed as nothing more than the result of a conflict of values between inner-city youth and the representatives of the dominant culture. Behavior that is regarded as bad by middle-class teachers is said to be the tolerated and expected behavior of the city slum—and, indeed, evidence of the adjustment of emotionally stable youths to their own subculture. Maccoby and her colleagues[5] have shown that this conflict of values does not exist. The residents of high delinquency areas were found to disapprove just as strongly of vandalism, thefts from stores, and fighting as those of low delinquency areas. Moreover, several studies have reported that maladjusted and delinquent children, even within working-class districts, are unpopular among their peers.[6,7] In the course of validating items of the Bristol Social Adjustment Guides,[8] I found that hostile boys were rated as popular only when they were outstanding at some sport. The chief reason for the prevalence of maladjustment and delinquency in disadvantaged areas is that the children living there are exposed to many more family troubles. Their parents are subjected to more severe stresses, and they break down in the same way as do animal populations under the stress of overcrowding: by attacking, driving off, or deserting their young.

Anyone who has had firsthand experience of these "sore spots" of our cities knows that they contain no homogeneous pattern of culture, but rather differing degrees of culture loss and personal breakdown—with many families maintaining their stability and standards amidst the prevailing disorganization and unruliness. All traditional cultures share a common core of human decencies. These include not doing physical injury to one's fellows—except for clearly defined ritual purposes (scarification, hockey violence, and so on)—not stealing from or insulting or hurting the feelings of other members of the community, obeying sexual taboos, and not wantonly challenging people's dearly held ideas. The children are trained not to do anything to disgrace their families and to be respectful to neighbors and authority figures. When inner-city children breach these universal canons of good behavior, it is because of the cultural disintegration of their families.

The behavior of children from traditional working-class localities does, nevertheless, tend to differ in certain respects from that of middle-class children. Not having acquired the habit of reading for pleasure nor having costly games to play with, they are often sent out into the street to play, where their rough-and-tumble games give them little training in reflective thinking or in controlling their impulses. Since their parents don't share the Protestant work ethic, diligence is not seen as a good thing in itself. However, none of these cultural differences impinge on the universal basic decencies listed above, and they would not be rated as signs of maladjustment.

This is not to deny that cultural factors are important in the causation of maladjustment. But maladjustment is not simply a cultural artifact arising from the way middle-class people view the behavior of working-class children. There is more maladjustment among the latter because its causes are linked to the general well-being of a community and the amount of stress to which its members are exposed. It will be seen that this stress-factor also applies to the innate emotional vulnerability underlying maladjustment. Maladjusted children create bad personal situations for themselves, and they fail to get the best out of life, even as measured by the restricted opportunities and expectations of an underprivileged social group.

THE NEED TO GET AT CAUSES

To help the maladjusted child, we need to recognize the symptoms and to acquire some knowledge of the various types of maladjustment and their origins. No significant progress was made in medicine until the working of the body—its nutritional needs and the noxious effects of viruses and bacteria—were understood. Until scientists understand the processes of change, progress is slow because it depends on chance discoveries. Faulty medical treatment that gave temporary relief or an illusion of improvement could be persisted in for centuries, until a better understanding of the body's working was achieved. The key to progress in the treatment of behavior disturbances is likewise an understanding of their causes.

For those who remain unconvinced of the need for this knowledgeable approach to maladjusted behavior, let us consider what may happen if people rely on instinct or the prevailing attitudes of their time. Both can be equally dangerous.

Consider first the dangers of relying on our "instinct." Having evolved as social animals, human beings are equipped with an array of instinctive responses that, under primitive conditions of existence, were of advantage for the survival of the group. Among the most powerful of these responses are those which held the group together: family affections, lifelong friendships, the attachment of a child to parents, community and group loyalties. Some of these instinctive reactions involve the sacrifice of a member of the group when that person is imposing too great a burden on the rest. The offending individual may first be warned by token gestures of disapproval—as when a parent loses his or her temper with a child. But if the "delinquent" persists in being a source of stress there comes a point where a heartless rejection takes over. The offender is driven out of the group or even physically attacked.

We shall see later that this reversion to primitive aggression against the source of stress supersedes normal affection, however deep or warm it may have been. The parent who physically attacks his or her child may otherwise be very kind and affectionate. More often the aggression takes a verbal form; but the expressions of rejection which result may be equally damaging because the child needs an unquestioned and permanent attachment to a parent. Rejection is just as instinctive and normal as affection. It was necessary for the survival of the group when existence was precarious. but it has now outlived its usefulness. Nevertheless, rejection remains a part of our human make-up, and, as in earlier stages of our development, it can be activated in times of frustration and stress.

In reading the case histories of delinquents committed to residential schools, the breakdown point—where affection and tolerance give place to rejection—can often be noted in the action of those who have had responsibility for the child. A former day school principal begins by affirming his belief in a child's essential goodness and expresses a determination to persevere. Then, suddenly, the tone changes; the erring member of the group has become an outcast. The youngster is rejected as an out-and-out bad type who, in the principal's opinion, needs a period of stern discipline in a correctional school.

I have observed the same sharp changes from friendship to rejection within the correctional school itself. A member of the staff befriends a youngster, and everything goes well for quite some time. But the youngster has been through the experience of being befriended and let down before, and cannot quite believe that this latest interest is genuine and permanent. He or she commits some provocative breach of discipline—or runs away and steals again—as a test of the staff member's loyalty. Nearly always, the instinctive response of the latter is, "After all I've done, this is how I'm rewarded. I'm finished with that child." The youngster is transferred to another, probably more secure, correctional school. Cynicism about the adult world is confirmed, and the youngster is given another push along the road to criminality. If the staff member had understood the true intention of the testing gesture, it could have been handled without emotional rejection.

Traditional attitudes sanctify this instinctive rejection. Ideas of original sin enable a parent to reject a child as "born bad." The principal of a school once described a child to me as being "just wicked." If ideas such as these lurk in peole's minds, it is easy—in moments of discouragement when the child has been more than usually troublesome—to make them the excuse for reverting to punitiveness and ceasing to try to offer any kind of emotional support.

WE CANNOT ESCAPE UNDERSTANDING

Apart from avoiding these emotional pitfalls, understanding the reasons for a child's maladjustment—what in medicine is called "diagnosis"—is the prerequisite for decisions about the form of treatment. The problem is knowing which of a number of possible explanations to accept. I remember reading in a case report that a boy of small stature became a "show off" and was led into delinquency by other boys because he felt inferior. That sounds like a plausible reason, until one asks why every boy of small stature does not become delinquent. Another child's tantrums and stealing are attributed to jealousy of a baby brother. But *all* older children don't become maladjusted on the birth of a brother or sister. Very few of the children who were hospitalized as infants become disturbed. We cannot dismiss any of these possibilities; if they are among the causes of maladjustment, we need to understand how they operate. We also have to be clear about what the emotional needs of children are and in what way the denial of them forces a child into abnormal behavior.

CONFUSION ABOUT THE CAUSES OF MALADJUSTMENT

There is, at present, little agreement on the causes of behavior disturbance. It is, therefore, not possible to write the usual sort of handbook that provides the reader with a convenient summary of established knowledge. This does not, however, absolve us from making an effort to piece together whatever knowledge of the causes of maladjustment may be available and to learn from our own observations. After all, we have plenty of data about behavior from our own experiences and from the experiences of people around us. As Jung[9] put it: "If concepts are lacking to us, facts are not; on the contrary we are surrounded—almost buried—by these facts. This is a striking contrast to the state of affairs in other sciences where the facts have to be unearthed." This is not to say that everyone can achieve a satisfactory understanding of behavior, whether normal or abnormal, merely by observing. One needs to know what to observe and how to piece it together. Nevertheless, knowledge gained from our own experience is more real to us—and a better guide to action—than that provided by a textbook. For this reason, I will present some of the observations of my students in Chapter 9 to show how it is possible to build an understanding of maladjusted behavior from our own experiences of other people's behavior. I am confident that the reader will find many parallels to these observations in his or her experience.

A NOTE ON TERMINOLOGY

This book is about children whose behavioral system is disturbed to the extent that they habitually act to their own disadvantage in everyday situations; these children can appropriately be called maladjusted. In referring to them, I use the terms "maladjustment" and "behavior disturbance" interchangeably. It is equally accurate to use the term "behavior disorder," although, to some people, this may be too suggestive of disease. In the United States, the term most often used is "emotional disturbance." It is, however, an inaccurate one. A child may be emotionally disturbed because of the death of a parent without becoming maladjusted. Moreover, some children are maladjusted in their behavior without being in the least emotionally upset.

I avoid the term "psychiatric disorder" because it conveys the impression that beyond a certain degree of severity maladjustment becomes something different, "psychiatric" in nature and akin to psychosis. According to the accepted definition, psychosis implies that a person loses all sense of reality and lives completely in a fantasy world. Children affected in this way are outside the scope of this book. Some maladjusted young people momentarily behave in a manner so crazy that if it were their habitual state they would qualify as psychotic; but even those who are most prone to such acts remain in contact with reality apart from such brief impulses, and their maladjusted behavior has its own logic, arising from the reality of their deprivation.

chapter two

Deprivation of affection

The most widely accepted cause of maladjustment in recent years has been the separation of child and mother during the early years. John Bowlby,[1] following the doctrine of Melanie Klein, became convinced that the first twelve months, or even the first six months, were critical for the child's ability to subsequently form ties of affection. Bowlby's thesis was widely taken up, and anxieties about letting children be taken into the hospital, even for a short time, became part of our modern folklore. I recall a mother and father coming to me with a deep sense of guilt because they had allowed their son to be hospitalized for a week when he was a baby.

The idea that separation at a critical early period causes irreversible damage was strengthened by what came to be known as "imprinting" in animals. A duckling hatched and reared among hens could not accept members of its own species. Lorenz found that goslings would attach themselves to the first moving creature that they saw after hatching, even if it were Lorenz himself. Overlooked was the fact that it is absolutely critical in terms of safety, for the young of wild geese or ducks, to keep close to their mother from the moment of hatching, and the first creature they see is almost inevitably their mother. Imprinting the image of their mother on them was thus an economical, instinctive means of insuring that they always followed her closely. Human infants, on the other hand, are not locomotive in the first six months of life. During the crawling stage the mother is normally there to bring the child back, and it is only when the child can toddle quite a distance that we see an anxiety to keep close to the mother. There was consequently no evolutionary need for imprinting—that is to say, a once-and-for-all attachment of the young to a specific mother figure—in the human species; despite eager search for such, no critical period for the development of human attachments has been found.

Early separation could not account for all behavior disturbance because not all disturbed children have suffered such separation. The concept was therefore broadened to include the quality of the affection that the infant received from the mother. So pervasive did this explanation become that where there was no actual evidence of lack of affection it was nevertheless assumed that the mother had been affectionally deficient in some subtle way. Needless to say, this addition to the folklore created widespread feelings of guilt among mothers and often had the unfortunate effect of inhibiting many of them even from correcting their child, lest the necessary withdrawal of love during a scolding do permanent emotional damage to the child. Nor was it only mothers who made this assumption that all young people's emotional problems could be traced back to a deficiency of mother-love in early childhood. Even the suicide of a college student, as I recall, was publicly attributed by a professional, without investigation of the case, to early deprivation of mother love. The distress of the mother in this instance can be imagined.

Because of the harm that can be done by an inaccurate folklore—and in order to gain a true understanding of the affectional needs of the child—a close examination has to be made of the evidence. This is all the more necessary because this folklore tends to be reproduced uncritically in student textbooks, along with the work of various authorities quoted in support of it, to an extent which suggests that their writers have not studied the original research reports.

The only studies which seemed to imply long-term ill effects of early separation were those of Goldfarb.[2] In one of these studies he compared a group of children who had been retained in an institution for up to three years with another group who had been placed in foster homes at an average age of fourteen months. He found that those who had been retained longer in the institution were more fearful and less spontaneous in their response to sympathy or approval. They were also less thoughtful in problem solving and more liable to quit a task that looked difficult. This fear of committing themselves must have been, at least in part, the reason for their considerably lower IQs. At the time, few people asked why one of the groups should have been retained in the institution so much longer than the other. Whereas nowadays attempts are often made to place even mentally handicapped children in foster homes, in those days it would have been the healthier, more attractive, and apparently brighter children who would have been placed first. Those retained longer would have been more likely to have been handicapped to begin with. The same weakness made Goldfarb's other studies inconclusive.[3,4]

The dramatic results reported by René Spitz for his *Hospitalism* study[5] occupy pride of place in many textbooks of introductory psychology. He compared two groups of infants: the "Nursery" children who, although inmates of an institution, were tended by their own mothers; and the "Foundling" children, who were kept in a hygienic isolation in another institution. Not only were the latter retarded in their developmental milestones, but their chief characteristic was "anaclitic depression," a general lifelessness. There was hardly a healthy child among them; of the 88 children, 23 were reported to have died before the age of two and a half years. The Nursery children, on the other hand, slightly increased their Development Quotients and nearly equalled those of children within the village population from which they came. These results set off a worldwide movement against the retention of infants in any kind of institution.

Pinneau[6] noticed many inconsistencies in Spitz's study. There was no definite statement of the number of children in each sample: the size of the Foundling group was reported variously as 61, 88, 91; the Nursery sample grew in the course of reporting from 69 to 123. The Developmental Quotients at the age of two years must have been given to different children, since the tests were not administered in the follow-up of the original sample. The main drop in the DQs of the Foundling group had occurred by the age of five months, but they were separated from their mothers only at around six months; and the fall between the ages of six and twelve months accounted for only 12 of the 52 point fall. Spitz reported an extreme susceptibility to infection and illness in the Foundling group from the third month on, that is, before they were separated from their mothers. He did not say why these children were given up to the institution, except for their mother's inability to support them. This is grossly untypical of a traditional culture, however poor. It is more likely that the Foundling group were seen by their mothers not to be thriving, and they were handed over to the institution in the hope of their having a better chance there. The Nursery group, on the other hand, were the illegitimate children of young mothers who came into the institution with them.

The two institutions served very different cultures; the Nursery being apparently in New York State, the Foundling somewhere south of the Rio Grande. Spitz refused to identify the institutions or even to indicate their approximate location. He maintained his refusal despite Pinneau's appeal to him to release their identity and his data to confidential nominees of a learned society. He also refused to name any of those who carried out the observations; Pinneau calculated that he must have needed at least twelve observers for the data he reported. When Pinneau continued to press him, Spitz accused Pinneau of being immoral because he was seeking to detract from the movement against early hospitalization. To this day, we do not know how Spitz got his data.

In Britain, it is the work of John Bowlby that first drew attention to the issue of separation. The hypothesis of his study, *Forty-Four Juvenile Thieves,*[1] was that early separation from the mother was likely to result in what he termed "Affectionless Character." Unlike Spitz, Bowlby published his case data with commendable frankness, in particular the criteria he used for identifying this type of child. The chief of these was "never since infancy having shown affection to *anyone.*" His other criteria follow: the child responded neither to kindness nor to punishment; the parents described the child as being "deep and unapproachable." Apparently he accepted any one of these three criteria as justifying a rating of "affectionless character," with the result that some of the children were judged to be thus even though they had shown themselves capable of affection. For example Betty (case 27) "became fond of her mother." She was, nonetheless, rated as affectionless because of her inability to express feelings, her nervous "woodenness" when corrected at school, her dreaminess, and her mixing with undesirables. Raymond (case 29) was said to be "affectionate and lovable, with a sunny disposition." But "his solitariness, aggressiveness, and complete unresponsiveness, combined with shameless truanting and pilfering" caused him to be rated as "a typical affectionless character." In fact, skipping school is typical of more than one type of maladjusted child, and all the 44 children were thieves. Norman (case 30) was said to be "a very affectionate child who liked helping his mother in the home . . . He was fond of his sister and played happily with her." But he was rated an "affectionless character" because he was "secretive, shameless in lying, and entirely unresponsive to punishment," and he had, moreover, a "sacred, lost look and a tendency to wander."

It is unnecessary to quote the seven additional cases in which the diagnosis of "affectionless character" is dubious. By this elasticity of definition, Bowlby was able to place in this category 12 of the 17 children who had been separated, but only two of the 27 who had not been separated. This gave him a highly significant result, to the effect that early separation tends to produce affectionless characters. If the ten contradictory or dubious cases had been given the benefit of the doubt, a slightly smaller proportion of the separated than of the non-separated would have been "affectionless," and no relationship between this supposed personality defect and early separation from the mother would have been established.

It is remarkable how uncritically these studies purporting to demonstrate the dire effects of early separation were accepted at the time. The first doubts appeared when Bowlby, with Mary Ainsworth,[7] published the results of a study which had been designed as a formal demonstration of the link between affectionless character and early separation. For their subjects they chose children who had spent some time in a tuberculosis sanatorium. But, it was found, their behavior differed from that of children who had not been separated only by their being more diffident, lacking in initiative and in concentration, and, with some of them, getting unduly rough during playtime. Bowlby and his colleagues admitted that their expectations had proved wrong regarding a deficiency of affection in these children. Not only was no disability in this respect noted, but at least half of these children mixed reasonably well and made friends readily.

At the time that Bowlby and Ainsworth published the above findings, I also reported mine[8] from a "bank" of 141 detailed life histories of educationally backward children, a large proportion of whom had been hospitalized in infancy. I chose the 25 who had been separated from their mothers for at least ten weeks during their first four years of life. In fact, the average length of their separation was over 18 weeks in the first year, and for the whole of the four years no less than 72 weeks, or about a third of their lives up to that point. Eight of these separated children were well-adjusted both at school and at home, were very affectionate and thoughtful towards their mothers, and helped them in the house. It should be noted that all had mothers who cared for them, although one was a cold woman who never kissed or cuddled her children.

The next group, again of eight, suffered from a handicap of temperament which I called "Unforthcomingness." They were timid, "mousey" children who "crept into their shell" when faced with anything or anybody strange. But they were not withdrawn in the sense of being affectionless; they were even more anxious to help their mothers than the first group. Nor could their unforthcomingness be put down to their early separation. I found that there were 51 children thus affected in the whole of my sample, only 20 of whom had suffered separation.

The third group were "unsettled" in that they showed mild signs of maladjustment. Examination of their life histories showed that they had had traumatic experiences or had suffered severe deprivation. One boy, a twin of a girl in the well-adjusted group, had been separated from his mother for nine months, during which time he had had his head shaved on account of ringworm without his mother or any member of his family being present. Another of these children was placed in an institution at three weeks of age, and he remained until he was three years old. His mother could not bear to visit him during most of this time but accepted him gladly when, on her marriage, he came to live with her. At home he was not a cuddly child: "You couldn't pick him up on your knee; he didn't want it." Her constancy won him over, but he would have terrific temper tantrums and get stubborn for really nothing at all. We shall later meet this tendency to revert to hostility in delinquent boys who never enjoyed stable maternal care.

The remaining four of these separated children were severely maladjusted, but in a way which was understandable in view of their severe and prolonged deprivation of a mother figure. One was a foundling child who had been in institutions all of her ten years of life; she showed that mixture of hostility and an anxiety for acceptance commonly found in permanently institutionalized children. A second girl was put into an institution for about two years when she was three and a half, her mother being an invalid who later died. After her institionalization, she was passed back and forth among various relatives, with the result that she became virtually unmanageable and could not be kept in a residential school, in a mental deficiency institution, or with a foster mother. Finally, an aunt by marriage was heroically determined to keep her. After a year of this new found security, the girl was very friendly and sought attention, but she became stormily defiant at the slightest provocation and stole frequently from the home. These are typical symptoms of hostility and loyalty testing that are frequently found among delinquent children. The acute deprivation which she had suffered conditioned her to be suspicious of any loving relationship.

The third of these children had been away from her parents—either in the hospital or evacuated—until she was six. Her maladjustment was also of the defiant, hostile type. Her repeated question, "If I am not a good girl will I have to go away?" revealed that she was subject to anxieties about being sent away again.

The common element in these three girls' lives was that they had no trustworthy mother figure during a large part of their childhoods, and they had to make do with such affection as was offered by whoever was in charge of them for the time being. Even then they were not affectionless; they had a burning need for affection alongside the rejection and hostility to which they reverted when corrected or on meeting an imagined rebuff. Their maladjustment was the imprint on them, not of separation at any critical point in their lives, but of their motherless state over the greater part of it.

The last of this maladjusted group came nearest to the "affectionless character" designation. He had trained himself never to seek sympathy, and so he did not cry when he hurt himself. His mother often threatened to have him put away—especially over his stealing, which he practiced shrewdly both at home and at school—but he showed no distress at the threat. He was one of those children who, although reputedly of dull intelligence, could "tell lie after lie and look you full in the face." We may ask what particular form of deprivation had carried him beyond the hostile, anxious type of maladjustment into a cold, unconcerned withdrawal. He had been hospitalized for two periods, amounting to six months, in infancy, but—as the mother unashamedly related to me in front of him— when he was six or seven she had "tried to get him away but we could do nothing about it . . . he was a drawback to me working in service." It was evident that, with her insensitivity, he must have heard all the details of the steps she was taking to get rid of him. Thus, his faith in her loyalty as a mother was progressively destroyed. Nevertheless, he helped her with the washing up, and swept the house for her; and he "starts to clear the table even before you have finished"—which shows that even for him the term "affectionless character" is inaccurate. We should speak rather of a state of affectional withdrawal, behind which may persist an anxiety for affection shown in signs such as the above.

The death blow to the idea that early separation produced "affectionless character" was administered by Siri Naess.[9] From the files of an Oslo social agency, she chose all those delinquent boys who showed its supposed symptoms, but she found that actually fewer of them had suffered early separation from their mothers than their non-delinquent brothers.

The error of the early researchers was to concentrate upon the fact of separation rather than to consider the wider effects of a child's being deprived of a loving and permanent relationship with a mother figure. In particular, their Freudian inspiration inclined them to give prime importance to separation in the first few months of life. This Schaffer[10] showed to be the least critical period as regards separation from a particular mother figure. From meticulous first-hand observation of how infants reacted to being placed in a hospital, he found that the effects were minor and very short lived in those whose stay had occurred before the age of seven months. On their return home, these babies tended to be unresponsive to their mothers because they were so preoccupied with scanning their surroundings; but this "strangeness" lasted, at the most, four days. Those over the age of seven months protested at being left in the hospital and were subdued or negative to the staff. On their return home, they clung to their mothers and cried whenever left alone, as if afraid of being deserted again. However, this emotional upset, although more serious in nature, lasted an average of only fifteen days.

Schaffer's study showing that the effects of single separation experiences were temporary, and the failure of the early workers to demonstrate dramatic effects in the form of "affectionless character" do not justify the opposite conclusion: that no ill can come of depriving the child of maternal affection and care. The nature and severity of the emotional damage could be assessed only by impartial and uncommitted inquiries. One of the most illuminating of such investigations was done by Hilda Lewis;[11] it was a study of children in a Child Care Reception Centre. The children had suffered a great variety of deprivation; separation, neglect within their own homes, the breakup of their families, and so on. Nearly half of those who had been separated, either temporarily or permanently, from their mothers under the age of five years were seriously disturbed, which compares with the 10-12 percent found in normal populations. But Lewis pointed out that in view of the long deprivation of maternal affection and care and the frequent moves from one substitute home to another, the bald fact of separation was not the main issue. Only *lasting* separation beginning before the age of two years was associated with a significant difference in behavior between the separated and the not-separated. Moreover, the most maladjusted children were those who first experienced separation after the age of five years.

One might say that the more aware a child is of being neglected, abandoned, or rejected, the greater the chance of that child becoming maladjusted. The older a child is, the more likely it is that such awareness will exist. The gravity of the problem of deprivation for children of all ages was demonstrated once more by Kellmer Pringle.[12] Among the 142 children in a large institution, aged 8 to 15 years, she found that, in the day school that they attended, 33 percent ranked as maladjusted, 32 percent as "unsettled," and only 35 percent as normal. The predominant form of behavior disturbance was anxiety for adult interest and affection, to which no less than 65 percent of them were prone. They were, in other words, deprived of that close and unquestioned attachment to parent figures that children of all ages need for healthy emotional and mental development.

To gain more exact knowledge of this attachment need, Kellmer Pringle, with her co-worker Bossio,[13] chose from the above group of institutionalized children eleven who were severely maladjusted and five who were notably stable. The majority of the 16 had spent virtually all their lives in children's homes, except for unsuccessful stays with foster parents. The maladjusted had come into public care at a younger age than the stable children, and all but two of them had been separated from their mothers before their first birthdays. Kellmer Pringle draws the following conclusion: "Never having experienced lasting love and loyalty from any adult, the child becomes unable to develop these qualities in his human relationships." Most of the maladjusted children had been deserted or abandoned. Fostering had been tried with five of them, but it had failed owing to their difficult behavior.

The most marked difference between the maladjusted and the stable children was that all the latter had had the benefit of regular contact with parents or parent substitutes, even though they could not live with them. This took the form of visits, being taken on outings and holidays, and receiving letters and parcels, the emotional value of which—in contrast to the traditional patronizing treat laid on by an organization—was that they were marks of the affection and thought of the *same* adults. In short, all the stable children experienced "a dependable, lasting relationship with a parent or parent substitute," whereas the nearest any of the maladjusted group came to this was a boy who was extremely attached to his mother and "lived for her infrequent letters and visits." But his typically hostile form of maladjustment showed that he had little faith in the permanence or depth of her loyalty.

The great importance of the deprivation studies was that although the original hypotheses had to be discarded they led to a more exact understanding of the emotional needs of children. In a classic study, Schaffer[14] destroyed the basis for the myth that attributed maladjustment, where there was no separation, to some subtle affectional deficiency in the mother. He divided his sample of mothers into two groups according to the way they interacted with their babies. The "personal" mothers provided much physical contact by picking up, kissing, cuddling, talking, cooing, and smiling. The "impersonal" mothers avoided contact by diverting the child away from them with toys or food. Schaffer's surprising finding was that the infants of the impersonal mothers developed the capacity to make specific attachments to individuals at just as early an age as those of the personal mothers. Having an impersonal mother does not, it seems, inhibit or delay the child's need for an affectional bond with a caring adult. Nevertheless, the babies did respond more intensely to the cuddling sort of mother. Moreover, they preferred those adults who interacted most warmly with them—not necessarily the parent who fed them. Theoretically, this is important because it shows that the children wanted a loving relationship for its own sake; it was not merely the result of conditioning to the source of food, as Watson, the behaviorist, maintained. Schaffer notes that from their earliest weeks the children themselves took the initiative in making social contacts. He therefore felt justified in assuming the existence of an inborn *attachment need*. The recognition of such a need in children of all ages is the key to understanding the greater part of maladjustment.

This attachment need takes different forms at each stage of the child's development. While helpless in the crib, the infant responds to endearments from all adults indiscriminately. From an average age of seven months, when mobility begins, the child develops specific attachments to the mother or to whoever reacts most lovingly, while at the same time becoming suspicious and frightened of strangers.[14] Later on, as the child's awareness of this need for adult support develops, the child comes to value the stability and permanence of the relationship. Demonstrations of love— in the form of endearments—are valuable; they give reassurance of the adult's attachment, and the child's response rewards the adult and tends to strengthen the bond. But it would seem that the essential thing is the constant attention, care, and reliability of a mother figure. The reader will recall that one of the well-adjusted children I studied had a mother who had never indulged in kissing or cuddling. In the Puritan culture of Scotland children would—at any rate, in my generation—have grown up without ever having had a kiss or any other open demonstrations of love from their parents. But because they were reared in stable families and had complete confidence in their parents, they grew up as emotionally stable people. In the next chapter we will further explore the nature of this need for secure attachment and the effects of the lack of it at all stages of growth.

chapter three

Reactions to degrees of deprivation

The histories of youths who, for a considerable period of their childhoods, had no adult whom they felt cared for them will be dealt with in this chapter. These youngsters were inmates of a correctional school where I was studying the causes of delinquency.[1] Since I ran an evening club for them, I could obtain frequent informal reports of their relations with the staff and other boys, and I was able to visit their homes or the homes of relatives. I obtained data on their behavior, feelings, and attitudes that enabled me to study the effects of various degrees of affectional deprivation. In these effects, we see the genesis and gain an understanding of some of the major types of maladjustment.

Middleton was the product of the chance encounter of an unmarried woman and a man whom she never saw again. From his birth until the age of five, he lived with her in an institution. When she had a second illegitimate child, she left the institution to go into service but did not take him with her. He then began to steal from an officer's cupboard.

Before he was six, he was transferred to another institution. At seven he was transferred again. During this time he saw enough of his mother "to break his heart" (as she put it) each time he had to part from her.

When he was nine, he was evacuated because of the air raids, and he spent the next four years with at least three foster mothers, until he was caught housebreaking and was committed to his first correctional school. While there he ran away several times. He spent two week-long leaves with his mother in the house where she worked as a maid. During his second stay he stole small articles from his mother's employer, and he was, consequently, not invited again. During the first part of this week he adopted the same dull, reserved manner toward his mother as he did toward other people, but during the latter part he "warmed up," showed himself affectionate, became quite talkative, and helped her with the housework. It was the same on her rare visits to him: during the first part he merely answered "Yes" or "No," but towards the end he talked more freely.

His behavior in this phase of his life demonstrates—as do all the other cases to be described—that a child's need for attachment to a caring adult cannot simply be put in cold storage. His separation from his mother at the age of five was so unbearable to him that he resorted to stealing. Because we lack information, we cannot say whether this was a matter of plunging into some activity which served to block the memory of the lost mother, a transfer of his grudge against her on to the officer, or a desperate attempt to bring about a change in his situation, perhaps by being restored to his mother.

We have to ask why—on the rare occasions that he was able to see his mother, instead of making the most of it and behaving well so that he might be allowed further visits—he stole from her employer and was unresponsive towards her. Obviously, since she had deserted him once, was prepared to leave him with other adults, and made rare contacts with him, she did not meet his need for a reliable mother figure. Moreover, the contact he had with her prevented him from forgetting her and kept his sense of deprivation alive. Consequently, his impulse was to break off the relationship with her altogether. He found it difficult to speak to her and behaved in a way to make sure he was not invited again. Nevertheless, he did not succeed in carrying out this strategy of rejection. When he was with her, the hope of having her as a mother again would be aroused; he warmed up to her and even helped her with her work—that latter being, as we shall see later, a standard symptom of mother anxiety. An interesting sidelight on his need for human attachment was that he had no such affectional inhibitions towards his young sister. He made a fuss over her and gave her piggy-back rides, which was quite unlike the withdrawn youth we knew.

He had extended his renunciation of social relationships to everyone around him. His dull, spiritless manner seemed devoid of any emotion. Nevertheless, he could not achieve a complete inhibition of his need. His eyes were frequently red, indicating that he had been secretly crying. When he was discovered preparing to run away again, he broke down and cried, confessing that he was going to look for his father. The possibility of the existence of a father who would cherish him had become an obsession. He felt sure there would be records, and he was going to find out where his father was. (The idealization of an absent father as a symptom of a child's lack of faith in the mother was common in my series of cases). In the meantime, we had arranged for him to have frequent meetings with his mother. In one of them, she told him the truth about his conception; this put an end to his quest, and he became much more friendly to everyone. He was, nevertheless, conditioned against getting involved in any close relationship. When the principal of the school took hold of his arm in a casual way—so that he could see better what he was showing him—Middleton jumped away like a frightened animal. Once, when he volunteered to run an errand for me, he added, "Just for something to do," as if he was ashamed to admit that he wanted to be friendly.

During the remainder of his time at the school he progressively accepted human relationships—after testing us out by another attempted or pretended runaway. After he joined the army, he visited the school on his leaves but again tested our interest in him by losing his return ticket and expecting us to pay his fare back. Unfortunately, he could never accept his mother. He didn't give her any of his army pay and, on a summer leave with her, stole from her, her friends, and from his younger sister. He was by no means a habitual thief; these thefts must be interpreted as his means of engineering a final break with her. Her previous desertion and neglect prevented him from putting his full trust in her. His reactions demonstrate the truth: that nothing less than full trust in a parent will satisfy a child's attachment need. So long as there are misgivings—as we shall see in subsequent cases—the child is tempted to put the parent's loyalty to the test. If the parent fails, the misgivings are replaced by rejection and provocatively hostile acts—stealing from the parents and their friends are the most common manifestation.

Not all the emotionally deprived wear their troubles on their faces.

Dixon did not, although he had suffered deprivation comparable to Middleton's. Except for being lodged in private homes during the war and a short spell in a foster home at five years, he had spent all his life in institutions, his mother having been for some years in a mental hospital. He had never been able to establish a permanent attachment to any parent figure. His grandmother had found him "too much strain" after a week. While living in a hostel he saved up for six weeks to visit an aunt, but when she opened the door and saw it was him she shut it again.

He had come to us from another correctional school where he had not gotten along with either the staff or the other boys. Besides stealing within the school, he had broken into houses in the town. He was a study in moods. One psychiatrist who interviewed him described him as "sulky, truculent, unfriendly, and anti-social. He shows no regret for his past lapses and feels he was justified in his conduct, as society has treated him so badly . . . a moral defective with definite psychopathic trends." Another psychiatrist disagreed. He interviewed him on the school sports day after he won some events, and he found him "eager to discuss his problems and most friendly." Dixon arrived at our school determined to make the most of us. I took a walk with him and I found him apparently happy and at peace with the world. He had few complaints, even against the people with whom he had quarreled. He was a pleasant companion, and I could easily have agreed with the second psychiatrist.

If any constant is to be found in the effects of deprivation, we have to ask why Middleton had withdrawn into a lifeless depression and hardly allowed himself to take any social initiative, while Dixon could be so open and amiable. The answer, in this case, is that Dixon was a handsome youth, while Middleton was not. People naturally took to Dixon, and he became adept at exploiting their good feelings. While working for a kindly farmer who had befriended him, he was rebuked for throwing a bucket of water over a pony. Dixon retorted, "Well, if that's the way you want it, I'll go," and he rode off on his bicycle. The farmer overtook him in his car and persuaded him to return, but Dixon never forgot the rebuke and did not remain long. He told me that the farmer had been unfair to him in not letting him have his car on unspecified business, which was actually to fulfill a probation appointment—he had committed some offense in the town.

Dixon eventually joined the Army and, like Middleton, spent some of his leaves at the school; during these leaves he expected the best treatment while causing inconveniences which made it seem as if he was challenging us to get rid of him. He could accept a friendly relationship while straining it almost to a breaking point. His long deprivation had made him irremediably suspicious of people. His lack of experience of any trustworthy parent figure at any time in his life had left him without hope of ever obtaining one. Other people were just to be taken advantage of. He had become an "affectionless character," not only from early deprivation but from a lifetime of it.

Unlike the stories of Dixon and Middleton, *Huntley's* story had a happy ending. He was the child of an adulterous relationship his mother had while still living with her husband. When she had another illegitimate child, her husband divorced her. Huntley was then two years old, and until he was seven—when he acquired a stepmother—it is not known who looked after him. It can be surmised that it was a woman to whom he became attached because, with the stepmother, he developed the classic symptoms of the hostility which arises from feelings of being deserted. He had a violent temper, was willfully destructive, and stole from his home and from houses of friends. Sent to a private school, he had to be removed because he misbehaved and stole. At about twelve years, he was put in what he described as a mental hospital. After a stay there his father consulted the State Office of Corrections about him; there, a woman official befriended him and placed him in a foster home. He felt deserted and unwanted at the foster home, "Just a thing in the house." Nevertheless, he grew fond of his foster father, and this enabled him to settle down with the family for about two years, until the foster father died. After a phase of difficult behavior, he spent seven months in the hospital with rheumatic fever. While there—because, like Dixon, he was a good looking boy—he got incidental mothering from the nurses. In his next foster home he acted out so much that he was transferred to a succession of hostels. In these and at his places of work he ran into difficulties—mostly because of his thefts—and he was finally committed to a correctional school for "Care and Protection."

Self-righteousness was Huntley's salient characteristic. Above all, he was indignant at being put among delinquents. He had "never stolen anything!" I listened to a long list of incidents in which he portrayed himself as the blameless youth who had been sinned against and exploited.

Meanwhile, the woman official from the State Office of Corrections continued to take a kindly interest in him. Whenever he got into trouble, he got advice and support from her. She must have kept alive in him some faith in humanity and hope for an eventual, permanent attachment. At our school he attached himself to his housemother and acted as her house helper. Then he found domesticity by working in the school kitchen, and he spent nearly all day with the woman cook and her five children. He became a hard and willing worker, extremely anxious to please and completely honest.

Huntley was fortunate in having two fairy godmothers. While he was in the school his half-sister traced his whereabouts and offered to give him a home when his time was up. At first—as would be expected with his degree of deprivation—he tried her patience, but she survived the test, and he settled down as a member of her family. When, after about some ten months, I visited him there, I was astonished to find how the sense of security that he got from being wanted had enabled him to exchange his pose of self-justification for one of humility. He no longer felt discarded and worthless and thus had no need to compensate by delusions of superiority. He even treated me to a long confession of his various dismissals and thefts.

The difference in the outcome, as compared to Dixon, was due, first, to the fact that Huntley had enjoyed secure attachment to an adult for periods of his childhood. These were not lengthy, but they provided some experience of affection upon which his later stability could be built. Second, two women had shown constancy towards him despite his trying ways. Moreover, both had taken initiatives in helping him when he was in trouble, although neither had any obligations to do so. His sister had even gone out of her way to find and give him a home! It was these practical proofs of interest and loyalty that counted.

Three further cases illustrate the effects of sudden, traumatic separation from a parent figure with whom an affectional bond had been established:

Crowther and his twin brother had been looked after mainly by their invalid father because their mother had a job and worked late. She was a prim and proper woman who claimed to have given her sons a sound religious training; but neither was affectionate to her. The father was the loving parent, and our twin was "daddy's pet." When they were eight and a half, the father died. The mother could not manage them, so she dressed them up—telling them they were going to the zoo—and took them to an institution. There, she handed them over to the superintendent and hurried off without even saying goodbye. She did not visit them until a year had passed—when our twin was in hospital with appendicitis. A few months later the boys spent six weeks at home, but they were "always out."

When the twins were about eleven, Crowther opted to go to a naval training school, although his twin brother, an exceedingly timid boy, preferred to live at home. But at fourteen, having failed the naval medical, Crowther found himself at home with his mother. He spent nearly all his time in the streets, sometimes staying out until the early hours of the morning. During this time he treated his mother inconsiderately. In the evenings he spent his time with a gang of boys who, like him, were bent on nuisance and excitement. It was for the excitement—not the money—that they broke into stores, an activity that they carefully planned. Finally Crowther was committed to our school because—in an act of bravado with his gang—he had broken the window of a railway carriage with a fire extinguisher.

Crowther was extremely surly and antagonistic upon his arrival. When I first interviewed him, he hardly bothered to answer me; instead, he devoted himself to a variety of compulsive fidgets. In the end, however, he could not resist the temptation to boast about his delinquencies and his work record. This consisted of getting jobs—and quickly getting fired for insolence—resenting orders, being late, or not showing up. His probation report confirmed that he had seven jobs in a month.

When I ask myself what meaning to attach to such a career of irresponsible and anti-social excitement seeking, I am reminded of many similar cases which are typical of the avoidance-excitement compulsion. It is the method children use to avoid the memory of events that might remind them of their state of deprivation. The incident that Crowther had to keep out of his consciousness was his abandonment in the institution when he thought he was only going to the zoo. Victims of such a compulsion are forced to occupy themselves with an endless succession of emotionally tense activities and fantasies: any kind of constant physical sensation, changes of scene, excessive expenditure on amusements, eating and drinking, and, above all, seeking excitement in troublemaking and delinquent adventure.

At home, the very presence of his mother was a constant reminder of the incident which epitomized her unreliability as a parent—the reason why he had to be constantly out of the house. His awareness of never having been cherished by her also produced in him feelings of inferiority;

he compensated for these feelings by boasting and displaying his don't-give-a-damn attitude towards adults.

In fact, Crowther—like most of the avoidance cases when removed from the reminders of their emotional plight—settled down quite well at our school. He readily joined my club and worked his way through a typical phase of childish silliness to the point where he could accept friendship. He was grateful for any favor shown, but he could never bring himself to ask for one. It was a long time before he could be persuaded to answer a greeting. His studied surliness, at the beginning, and his picking and biting and hair twisting were more ways of avoiding social relationships than genuine antagonism. He was by no means an "affectionless character." At home, he had been kind to his imbecile sister; he wanted to take her for walks and gave her sweets. When she was put in an institution, he cycled sixty miles to visit her.

Ferguson, also born out of wedlock, was accepted by a kindly foster mother with a view to adoption; however, this was not sanctioned owing to the poor state of her home. He was introduced to his real mother at the age of eight, but he refused to believe her to be so. Nevertheless, the incident must have been traumatic because he became difficult in the foster home, and, at just under twelve years—having been convicted of housebreaking—he was sent to a junior correctional school for "Care and Protection." When he was fourteen and of wage earning age, his true mother claimed him. But he repeatedly ran back to his foster parents, who, however, could not be cajoled into letting him stay with them; they paid his fare back to his mother. Finally the Court restored him to them.

This should have been a happy ending to his troubles, but the fact remained that his foster mother had formally abandoned him. It made no difference that she was only doing her legal duty as she saw it. He became an "enfant terrible," tormenting her by stealing money from her purse, remaining out all night, staying away from work, and living at her expense without contributing to his keep. Nevertheless, he expressed great fondness for her, and he was determined to adopt her name when he was twenty one. He came to me in great distress and asked me to write to her because he had not heard from her for a week. In fact, he had just received a parcel from her which he had not acknwledged; he counted on extracting another by pretending it had not reached him. As I had promised him, I went to see her later in the week, only to find that the previous evening he had run away, leaving her home prior to my arrival. This was only the day after she and her daughter had come to see him. On that visit he stuffed himself at their expense, complaining after each of a succession of meals that he was still hungry. To raise the money for his railway fare for the planned escape, he wheedled money out of them—he said he needed money to go to the movies and to a football game, neither of which privileges were allowed him as a newcomer to the school. Finally he asked about the next station on the line so he could swindle the railway company.

It was evident that this callousness and the planned crookedness of his strategies had not emerged overnight. His confidence in the gullibility of the dear old foster mother must have grown over many years of manipulating her. If he had merely been a thoroughly spoilt boy he would have looked after his own interests better and would have known how far to go. That his delinquency dated from his first encounter with his mother is evidence that his fear of being abandoned by his foster mother dated from then. The early housebreaking and his later inability to settle down with her point to an avoidance compulsion. The fact that he plagued her— starting with his attitude change after the traumatic "mother" episode— seemed a combination of loyalty testing and hostility. By the time we knew him he had succeeded in killing all his finer feelings towards her— except in hypocritical avowals of love. His callousness was his defense against the threat of further abandonment. Although he was not withdrawn in a literal sense—he was aggressive and importuning as well as being a braggard—he was withdrawn in the sense that he had inhibited his need for affection and turned it into imposition.

Fisher told me that he had spent the past thirteen years—that is, all except his first three—in an orphanage. He made no complaints about his life there. He had never known life in a family, he said, and tried to imagine what it was like. Only reluctantly did he admit—when asked pointedly—that he had a brother and sister; he knew of their existence only because the superintendent of the institution had told him. Asked if he would like to meet them, he replied, after a pause, "I don't think so. I'd rather stand on my own." His file stated that between the ages of four and thirteen he had lived with foster parents; he was subsequently evacuated but could not return to them after the war owing to bomb injuries they suffered. His story of continuous instititionalization was so real that I wondered if there could have been some confusion in the records. But inconsistencies appeared. He later admitted that his brother and sister used to visit him in the orphanage, and that he had seen both within the past year.

His behavior was typical of a youth who was avoiding unpleasant memories. He simply could not sit in a chair and read a book; he had to always be playing an active game like table tennis. He disliked my evening club because it was too quiet. When he heard other boys talking about their mothers and fathers he turned away.

When he let it slip out that he knew his sister's address, I decided that the first step was to bring the two together (to help him face up to the memories he was avoiding). Unlike youths dominated by some of the more extreme avoidance compulsions, Fisher had not succeeded in achieving a complete amnesia. "I think I ought to tell you," he blurted out, "that I have lived in a home before" (meaning family, not institution). Only I didn't want to think about it." He told me of his foster mother; he had become attached to her as to a mother, and he even called her "mother." He also called her husband "father," and while at school went by their name.

It was only since his return from being evacuated that he was put in an orphanage, which was near his foster parents' home. When he tried to visit them, he found the house destroyed by the bombing. A few weeks later he discovered their whereabouts from a neighbor and visited them for a time, but because his foster mother was still suffering with her nerves she could not take him back. It was at this point that he tried to forget her.

When we contacted the foster parents they not only agreed to take him back but actually found a job for him; they did not realize that he had been committed to a correctional school. But he was nervous at renewing the relationship. What if they discovered that he had been a thief? He could not even bring himself to write to them. After I made another visit to the foster parents they sent him a present, said they knew all and were prepared to forgive him. He spent his next leave there and finally settled down with them when his time at the school was up.

Although he was a sad, depressed boy, Fisher did not show the hostility or callousness which marked the others in this group. Once again, we see how the years during which he enjoyed an affectionate relationship—one he had regarded as permanent—made it possible for him to reaccept those who had cared for him during the greater part of his childhood. Moreover, he could excuse them for not taking him back after his evacuation; they had, after all, suffered shock from being bombed and having their home destroyed. His doubts were similar to those of a child who had been conditioned to anxiety by early deprivation. He had, in effect, been neglected by his mother during his first two years, and he had lived with two foster mothers by the age of five. It was only with the third that he settled down and found security.

THREE MAJOR REACTIONS TO DEPRIVATION

In this chapter we have detailed the three major reactions to deprivation, defined as the denial of the child's need for secure attachment to a loyal and caring mother figure. They constitute some of the major forms of maladjustment. However—as we shall see when we deal with emotionally deprivating family situations—they do not arise only where there is formal physical separation from the loved mother figure.

These reactions can be related to the length and poignancy of the deprivation. Children who have never enjoyed the loving care of a mother figure for any considerable period of their lives are nearly always in a state of severe *withdrawal* by the teenage years. These youngsters shy away from any human attachment because they lack confidence in its permanence and they fear being abandoned once again. This state amounts to a denial of the need for affection. At the same time they nurse a grudge against humanity on account of their deprivation. In spurning all affectionate relationships, they treat callously those who have shown kindness. This lack of a sense of human fellowship is seen in their immoral behavior towards people in general. Nevertheless these youngsters are not emotionally at peace with themselves in their withdrawal, nor stable in their self-denial, because the stress of continually inhibiting their need for attachment exhausts all their nervous resources. Their attitude to others may therefore reach the condition of paranoia—although it is by no means only withdrawn people, as thus defined, who are subject to this condition. They may even find an outlet for their thwarted need in a handicapped child or an animal because they feel safe from rejection. Nevertheless, we are not inferring that other people who love handicapped children or animals do so as a substitute for human attachments; they are probably following more normal, instinctive impulses common to the human race.

Hostility, the second of these major reactions, arises when these children are so deeply apprehensive about being rejected or abandoned by the parent figure—regarded as the permanent object of attachment—that they can bear the uncertainty and the anxiety no longer. They therefore set out to hasten the feared breach by behaving in a way calculated to bring it about. This takes the form of provocative nuisance, which includes stealing within the family and from the parents' friends. As an intermediate phase, these children may use acts of annoyance to test the loved parent's loyalty; they want to reassure themselves that the parent will stick by them whatever they do. Hostility—in this active sense as a reaction against construed disloyalty—is found only when the child has been able to build up a loving attachment to an adult which had been considered permanent. This hostility can be likened to the fury of the jilted lover.

Avoidance, as a form of disturbed behavior, consists in a compulsion to seek exciting and absorbing diversions as a means of forgetting the loss of the loved parent figure. It usually centers around the attempt to blot out of the memory some traumatic incident which epitomizes the loss; other shocks occurring at the same time may also be "forgotten" in the process. The sudden appearance of the true mother—which threatened the boy's hitherto secure relationship with his foster mother—and the discovery that his former home had been bombed, are examples of such traumatic happenings.

chapter four

Countermeasures
against
deprivation

In our present state of community disintegration—where there are often
no longer other branches of a family willing to give a home to youngsters
left without parents—it is unavoidable that some children have to be taken
into public care. We have, therefore, to consider how the dangers of
deprivation can be minimized. Apart from the possibility of eventually
reuniting these children with their own parents, this can be achieved only
by providing substitute parents who would be as caring and as *permanent*
as true parents. If this is not done, the continued deprivation—in the form
of inadequate and temporary adult-child relationships—is likely to result in
one of the major forms of behavior disturbance exemplified in the
previous chapter.

It may be argued that our present childcare services are not capable
of guaranteeing all deprived children this chance of new and more permanent parent figures. This does not prevent us, however, from establishing the principle and showing it to be justified both from a humanitarian and an economic point of view. In relation to the latter, it should
be realized by the taxpaying public that one wrecked life can—when the
expenses of maintaining unemployable individuals, mental health care,
incarceration, and so on are added up—cost the community as much as the

total salary of a social worker. The social worker has, consequently, to succeed in setting up only one child per year with permanent substitute parents to earn his or her salary. This equation must be borne in mind when the feasibility of the following proposals is considered. It shows that efforts to cut social service costs are nothing less than short sighted extravagance. To this must be added the observation that one damaged personality sets the pattern for further generations of deprived and emotionally abused children.

TEMPORARY REFUGE

The arrangements made for the care and treatment of a deprived child depend on the circumstances of the deprivation. The first question to be asked is whether the true parents might be in a position to give the child a secure and permanent home in the not too distant future. It may be that a series of misfortunes has reduced the true parents to a state of emotional breakdown in which they become intolerant of the child and may possibly do him physical harm. In such a crisis, the child has to be removed immediately, but the childcare worker would not be justified in severing the child permanently from the parents. A variety of situations in which parents break down or abandon or reject their children are described in the next chapter. A large proportion of these situations are reparable. We consequently need to have a certain number of residential schools, group homes, or hostels where deprived children can find refuge and have time to recover from the emotional stresses to which they have been subjected.

Where there is a reasonable chance that the child may be restored to his or her parents, placement with a foster mother may cause difficulties later. One of the recurrent sources of emotional conflict in the delinquent youths I studied[1] was the formation of a primary attachment to the foster mother during wartime evacuation; on their return, they found it difficult to accept their own mothers.

It cannot always be decided at the time of the removal of these children whether they may one day be able to return to their families. Their rejection or abuse could have been due to a temporary mental breakdown of an otherwise loving parent. If the parent's health and circumstances improve there may be little risk of a recurrence of the trouble. A state of mutual hostility may have developed between parent and child which culminated in the latter's running away and/or behaving in a provocative manner in order to secure removal from the home. Children who are very attached to their mothers may be driven to distraction by an illness—or possible complications of childbirth—and the fear of losing their mothers cause them to resort to irresponsible, excitement seeking escapades. The possibility of relieving the family's problems and giving the parents insight into the reasons for the maladjustment of such children cannot be judged by the violence of the upset.

The social worker needs time to work with the family and bring about a reconciliation of parent and child. This reconciliation should, in effect, be the prime objective in all cases—except those in which it is judged to be out of the question. Only when it becomes apparent that the parents are incapable—despite the efforts of the social worker—of providing a secure and loving home, should a decision be taken to place the child with an alternative parent figure.

WORKING WITH THE PARENTS
DURING THE CHILD'S ABSENCE

The first steps in a program for restoring a child to the family is a careful diagnosis of the reasons for the estrangement, based on the objective indications described in Chapter 7. The parents should then be led to an understanding of the reasons for the child's anxiety and consequent maladjustment. Such insight may enable them to avoid situations and desist from statements and actions which have undermined their child's faith in them; it also gives them a way of excusing the child's behavior and of reaccepting the youngster without feeling that they are denying their own principles. The parents' response to such counseling will indicate the genuineness of their concern for the child. They should also receive practical guidance in healing the breach—if such has come about—by making frequent visits, writing letters, and sending an occasional parcel of goodies. They should also be encouraged to discuss with their child the arrangements they are making for his or her eventual return: buying a new bed or a bicycle or making inquiries about employment.

In short, the time that a child is away from home in temporary residential care should be regarded not as a punishment—or simply a holding operation for lack of any better solution—but as a stage in a carefully thought out plan of rehabilitation and reconciliation. It requires the constant attention of a social worker to the needs of each particular child; this attention should be on a par with the medical care given to a person suffering from a long-term illness. This can be done only if the childcare worker has a small case load—no more than ten children. The economy of such a case load has already been argued.

NEED FOR A CONTINUITY OF CASEWORK SUPERVISION

There should be a continuity of supervision by the same childcare worker during the period of residence and after the child's return home. The child should get to know the childcare worker by having natural opportunities to talk with him or her alone, such as on a walk or a visit to the movies with a meal to follow. By such contacts, the child may come to regard the childcare worker as a source of continuous support. The case of the boy quoted in the previous chapter, who was befriended by a government official, was only one of the many cases in my experience where such support has buoyed up a child's feeling that there is someone who cares. The principal of the correctional school in which I worked had a large "family" of young men who periodically wrote to and visited him after they left. It does not matter that the uncle or aunt figure is a professional whose job it is to care for insecure young people.

The need for a continuity of casework care is underlined by a glaring weakness—one might say an inexcusable folly—of our present system of institutional treatment: returning a child to the same depriving situation that provoked the breakdown in the first place. Welfare officers responsible for the after care of hundreds of youngsters, on their return from residential schools have not the time to probe into family tensions or the causes of the maladjustment. Indeed, a child should not be returned home until the source of the insecurity has been discovered and the childcare worker is confident that it has been overcome, and—where there was a breach—until parent and child have reaccepted each other. These processes take time; first, because the true state of the family relationships may be revealed only after some new crisis prompts one party or the other to drop all reserve and admit the difficulties; and second, because during the period of the child's problem behavior at home the attitudes of the parents may have hardened, and the child may bear a grudge which takes time to dissipate. When I worked with members of the staff of the Kingswood Training School near Bristol, one of them made an observation which summed up the situation in such cases: during the first year of the boy's stay at the school little progress could be made in reconciling him with his parents, but thereafter one party or the other would begin to soften, and by the end of the second year the mutual reacceptance would be complete and the boy could be returned to his home with confidence. In such cases, a shorter stay in the school would almost certainly have been followed by an early reversion to deviant behavior.

AIMS OF TEMPORARY CARE

The main aim of temporary residential care should be to discover the reasons behind the child's maladjustment so that the basis for a treatment program can be established. These may be chiefly of a situational character. The majority of boys who have resorted to delinquency or other bad behavior as a means of escaping from an emotionally intolerable home situation quickly become normal again in the structured life of a residential school. Although they may have stolen regularly while at home and skipped school and work, once they are in the new surroundings—where their anxieties no longer press on them—they become honest and trustworthy. Their behavior is so exemplary that they are sometimes given an early release on the grounds that residential treatment is unnecessary. Within a few weeks they are back in school with an addition to their record of housebreaking or personal violence.

Other young people taken into residential care are conditioned to hostility and distrust, and they are still obsessed with their anxieties or the acting out of their anger against humanity. Bettelheim[2] has enunciated some important principles for the rehabilitation of such children. The primary aim of his school was to provide the child with continuous experiences of adult kindness and helpfulness in the course of the daily routines. The members of the staff studied each child's needs and emotional state and aimed to come up with some practical demonstration of concern. Bettelheim stressed the situational nature of the treatment and, although a Freudian in his philosophy, regarded formal treatment sessions as unnecessary and possibly harmful. He argued—correctly in my opinion—that a child's feelings about the world emerge more easily through the realities of everyday life than in symbolic, fantasy situations. Nevertheless, it does sometimes help to discuss a child's behavior and feelings with him. Youngsters can continue under the influence of an obstinate compulsion to behave in a certain way without realizing that they are thereby thwarting their own needs. A boy may be desperately anxious for the friendship of other boys, yet unwittingly alienate his companions by bragging in order to try to appear important to them. It is a good idea for every young person in a residential school to have a mentor to whom he or she can come for guidance. The mentor should preferably be someone who has no formal teaching or supervisory duties in the school. My position as a club leader was ideal in this respect. The club members came each evening—or whenever they wanted to—and could talk with me informally or ask me favors such as buying things in the town for them, or writing to or visiting their parents. It also gave me opportunities to observe their behavior; when a boy was depressed or unduly hyperactive, it was usually a harbinger of trouble.

Another important aspect of Bettelheim's situational therapy is his belief that young people will regain confidence in people by learning to get along with their companions. Many of those who bring anti-social attitudes with them into the school may need help in building peer relationships. A child conditioned to distrust by many experiences of rejection is apt to misconstrue insignificant happenings and break off an incipient friendship without verifying the intention of the other person. Consequently, the mentor has to keep an eye on the growth of the child's friendships and be ready to help him or her over periods of strained relationships.

THE FORM OF TEMPORARY RESIDENTIAL CARE

It was pointed out above that temporary placement in a foster home can lead to difficulties when the child returns to his or her own family. Some type of residential school—or hostel, if the young person is of working age—is therefore indicated. Children can indeed be very happy in a boarding school, especially because of the opportunities it provides for friendships with peers and experience of caring and devoted adults. I agree with Bettelheim that staff members should not become substitute parents in the full emotional sense because this also leads to difficulties when the child has to leave; it may also cause unpleasant incidents arising from jealousies and disappointments. Rather the child should have a perception of at least one staff member as someone to be turned to without fear of rebuff when difficulties arise; this person should be someone who shows a daily interest in the child's welfare.

Bettelheim also has some very important things to say about the persona that the staff member should project to the children. I cannot do better than quote his words: "In order to give the child back his security, which depends on the fact that adults can protect, and if necessary control him, all the adult at the school has to do is be himself and act in line with his age. By doing just that, he provides an image for the child to emulate. At the same time he restores the child's security which derives from his being cared for by a strong and effective adult." Staff members who lower themselves in the children's eyes by allowing the children to treat them disrespectfully—either verbally or physically—cannot meet the child's need for a strong, protecting adult.

The size of the residential school is unimportant, provided the children are grouped in small units of six to eight under the care of their special adult. Ideally, the buildings of the school should reflect this form of organization; the group should have some of their meals together and share a sitting room and a leisure time room. The bedrooms should accommodate not more than four children. This number enables friendships to develop and forces everyone to tolerate the foibles of the others. Beyond that cliques can develop, individuals can become isolated, and bullying can occur.

DISCIPLINE AND ROUTINES WITHIN THE RESIDENTIAL SCHOOL

Recognizing that the emotional resources of the maladjusted child taken into residential care are at a low ebb, Bettelheim pursued a policy of removing all possible sources of tension or conflict. The children in his school were not expected to do any household chores or to attend classes. In fact, they were never made to do anything, not even to eat or to go to bed at a set time. For the kind of obsessionally disturbed children who came to his school, such a "frustration free" regime may often be necessary because these children interpret every attempt to bring order into their lives as further evidence of adult hostility and bullying. This, however, must be viewed as emergency treatment for the severest cases, akin to hospital treatment. In the correctional school to which I was attached, it was sometimes necessary to put youngsters who were emotionally at the end of their tether in the sick room for a few days. There they would have physical rest and the companionship of adults who were not trying to regiment them. For such young people, the alternative of isolation can only add to their hatred of the human kind.

Apart from these extreme cases of disturbance, which verge on psychosis, an ordered daily routine should be part of the treatment, and it will be accepted, provided it is seen as sensible and designed for everyone's good. The youngster who has yearned for a homelike atmosphere will appreciate kitchen duties or even looking after young children. Others may find emotional satisfaction in looking after animals, even if it means getting up at 5 a.m. to milk the cows. Regular duties and responsibilities also act as a preparation for subsequent life in school and employment. The danger of a philosophy of permissiveness—exemplified by A. S. Neill—is that it may actually give children false expectations of the world they will find outside the institution.

It goes—or should go—without saying that corporal punishment for children who are victims of emotional abuse to the extent that they vent their hostility on people in general, and whose nervous resources are so low that they are prone to uncontrolled outbursts, is not merely harmful but amounts to cruelty. Provided the discipline is community oriented—in the sense that it is seen as a means of ensuring respect for everyone's welfare and happiness—any misconduct can be treated as a temporary breakdown of an individual's social controls. The reasons for it should be gone into and discussed with the offender. In doing so, important and often surprising reasons for the bad behavior may come to light. The following is a striking example of this: Paul was a handsome youth with a fine singing voice who, despite efforts to befriend him and to develop his talent, was a continual nuisance in a correctional school; this was due to his unprovoked outbreaks of bad temper, about which he was himself mystified. All he could tell me was that the windows of his boarding house which faced on to the recreation yard made him feel like running amok. They seemed to remind him of something, but he could not recall what. I went to inspect the windows and saw that they had unusually small panes. He could not admit any anxiety concerning his life at home, but I went there to find out what I could. As I approached the house I saw that its windows had exactly the same small panes. From his decrepit old father and his stepmother I learned about the traumatic event that the windows reminded him of. During a quarrel, his stepmother, who wanted him out of the way, told him that his mother had gone around with other men and that one of them was his real father. The old man was too taken aback and confused to deny it. Thereupon, the boy ran out of the house and committed a series of robberies. But the affair had a happy ending. By family resemblance it was established that the boy was the son of the old man. With this reassurance and with bringing the event into his consciousness, the boy settled down and completed his time at the school without further trouble.

Harry was a seven-year-old boy who was prone to similar violent outbursts. At our Center for Educational Disabilities in Guelph, to which he was referred, he would suddenly sweep whatever materials he was using onto the floor, attack other children or fly at the teacher and bite her; these biting attacks occurred once or more at every session. The remarkable thing was that in between these outbursts he was a sensible, affectionate child and a very good worker. They were related to a particularly distressing home situation. The father was serving a term of imprisonment for beating up the boy's mother. From the prison the man wrote letters to his own mother describing the beatings he was going to give his wife when he got out. The paternal grandmother, who took her son's part, visited the mother and read the letters out loud in front of the boy. These were the events that he was trying so desperately to black out of his memory; the only way he could do so was to commit some mad, violent act when something reminded him of the awful prospect of his father's return. He confirmed our suspicions about the cause of his outbursts one day by going into a dreamy, distracted state and talking about his obsessing fear. After he was placed with a foster mother and had learned to accept the staff of the Center, the outbursts ceased.

Not all persistent bad behavior has such a dramatic story behind it as these two examples. Nevertheless, it has to be borne in mind that children only resort to such behavior when they are intensely unhappy and driven to misbehave by a burning resentment or by the necessity of blocking out intolerable memories. Children normally want to keep in good standing with their peers and with the adults who are in charge of them. Bad behavior thwarts both these natural needs. Even though a child may have had little exposure to a disciplined way of life, as soon as he realizes the penalties of bad behavior he mends his ways. It can thus be reasoned that those who persist in bad behavior are under some compulsion to do so. The discovery and removal of its causes and—if he is old enough—helping the young person gain insight into his or her unconscious compulsion, are more effective ways of dealing with bad behavior than harsh punishment.

THE PERMANENT CARE OF THE DEPRIVED CHILD

Where there is no prospect of restoration to the true parents, the aim should be to establish the youngster in another family on a permanent basis. In borderline cases, where there is still a remote possibility that the true parent may eventually be able to claim the child back, there should be some legal provision to prevent the child from being removed from a foster parent with whom a firm attachment has been formed. In such a situation, the child's own wishes—if he or she is old enough to decide—should be the decisive factor. We should consider the right of the child to choose, rather than the right of the true parent to claim the child as a possession.

The repeated shifts from one foster mother to another, of which one reads in the case records of some maladjusted and delinquent children, should make us realize that our present practice of fostering should be reviewed. This practice consists of finding a motherly woman and persuading her to take in one or more children, possibly with little greater remuneration than covers their keep. Therein lie weaknesses. The first is that instinctive mothering works well in the case of the normal child, who responds to the offer of love and does not unduly burden the mother—but alongside it there are equally instinctive tendencies to reject the unrewarding or tiresome child. The second is that since most deprived children are either illegitimate or the product of unstable and stressful marriages,[3],[4] they are more likely to be unhealthy and to suffer from habit and behavior disorders. Many of them will be impaired in more than one way. In short, they can be the kind of unrewarding, stress-inducing children who evoke rejection rather than motherly acceptance. These represent the bulk of children who are shifted from one foster mother to another, and they finally end up in an institution.

Natural, untutored maternal feelings cannot therefore be relied upon when the foster mother has to cope with a maladjusted child. They have to be supplemented by an objective, professional attitude based on an understanding of the child's condition. A foster mother requires training for her vocation. The usual academic course would obviously be inappropriate, but it should be possible to design a part-time course, taken non-residentially, in which the teaching is oral and informal. This type of course would have to prepare the would-be foster parent for a period of difficult behavior with a child who has already suffered emotional abuse. She must be briefed not to take a serious moral view of lying and stealing but to see such as the result either of the child's anxiety about rejection or resistance to the acceptance of a loving relationship. Above all, she must be prepared for her devotion to be put to a severe test by some flagrant and uncalled for actions on the part of the child; and she must expect this behavior just when everything seems to be going so well. She will also have to be trained in providing the child with constant reassurance, both verbally—"You're my very own child," "When you're big and grown up you'll be able to look after me like I'm looking after you now,"—and by practical demonstrations of the permanence of the child's membership in the family—introducing the child to relatives as the new son or daughter and (in the case of an older child) adding items of furniture to the bedroom, letting him or her choose decorations, fixing up hobby apparatus, and so on. The qualifying examination for the foster parent's certificate should also be oral, and it should cover these confidence building strategies as well as techniques of household management for a large family. Once qualified and in practice, the foster mother would be expected to attend regular seminars with her colleagues in which their current work and problems are discussed.

A foster mother thus trained would naturally expect a salary, but this type of care would still be much less expensive than maintaining the children in an institution. The number of foster children in any one home would, needless to say, depend upon the foster mother's experience and record of previous success, and her age. If she has three or four at any one time, it would be better if they were spaced out in age as a natural family would be. Even if the foster children could not be legally adopted, they ought to take her name. It would be expected that the foster children would maintain the same ties with the foster parents and each other for life, as if they were natural sons and daughters.

chapter five

Maladjustment arising from defective parent-child relationships

When we come to consider the maladjustment of children living with their own parents, two sources of confusion have to be cleared up. The first is that some types of maladjustment are best described as handicaps of temperament. Not only are the parents not to blame for them, but one has sometimes to admire their patience and fortitude in continuing to care for a child whose behavior may be extremely trying. It is, nevertheless, not possible to make a clean division between maladjustment arising from temperamental handicap and that arising from the family situation. A constitutional abnormality of behavior can so perplex and exhaust the parents that they reject the child or give way to expressions of exasperation which the child construes as rejection. In the cycle of worsening child-parent relationships which is started in this way the child displays the typical reactions to deprivation.

The second source of confusion is that not all undesirable behavior within the family is maladjusted by our definition. The domestic misbehavior of many adolescents is usually a bid for independence and sometimes for dominance. They signal to their parents that they resent their activities being supervised as when they were younger. It is hard for parents to abandon former methods of care and control and, aware of the young person's inexperience, transmit to them some of their own life's experience. On the other hand, the typical adolescent lives intensely in the present, and this includes a need for acceptance by age peers. The resulting friction—which may take the form of a running battle lasting some years— is therefore an understandable phase in the growing up of a normal family. In traditional cultures it was usually avoided by providing accommodation outside the parental home for the adolescents and making adults other than the parents responsible for their education—of which the British private school system is a good example.

Nevertheless, this phase of conflict seldom results in mutual rejection and the estrangement of the adolescent from the parents because, in a normal family, both sides sense when they are approaching the danger point. Just when the young person seems to be quite "impossible," and the parents are near the end of their patience, he or she makes a peace overture. The truth is that despite their anxiety to conform with their age group, adolescents are fundamentally more concerned about retaining the support and affection of their parents.[1] The process can be likened to difficult and bitter negotiations in which both parties realize that they have to reach an agreement. Adolescents who push the bargaining furthest are the one's who have been able to dominate and try their parents over the years with impunity. Such young people are over-secure to the extent that they become selfish and unfeeling. Their parents are sometimes bewildered when they discover that their domestic source of strife is, outside the home, "the sweetest person you could imagine." The question on their lips is, "Why can't our child behave like that towards us?"

Nevertheless, there is some element of danger in this bad behavior which is reserved for the family situation. The mental health of the family depends on the mental health of the parents. If one of them breaks down under the strain of the child's behavior, that parent is likely to revert to defensive rejection. The distraught mother threatens to clear out, and even be reduced to a state where she threatens to murder the child. The latter's faith in the parent is destroyed, and he or she answers by hostility or one of the other reactions to deprivation. A further danger is that young people who have found that they can get their own way by playing on the nerves of their parents risk becoming conditioned to these tactics in their future marriages; this can result in disaster, especially if both marriage partners are this way.

In adolescent girls there is another instinctive tendency that must also be accounted as normal, unless carried too far. In nearly all traditional cultures—so far as we can go back in history and observe primitive societies—the woman moves into her husband's family group on marriage. Up to marriageable age—that is to say, thirteen or fourteen—she has enjoyed the close affection and shelter of her own mother. If this attachment remains the primary one of her life, she will not be able to bear the parting without distress, and she may refuse to leave the parental home or may run back to it again. The instinctive way of breaking an affectional relationship that is unrewarding is to substitute for it a highly emotional antipathy and an urge to get as far away as possible from the former loved one. This is the essence of the hostility which children direct against their parents when they become convinced that the parents wish to get rid of them. It is a self-banishing reaction; children who feel rejected try to terminate their anxiety by killing their erstwhile affection. Likewise, the instinctive preparation for the physical separation from her parents that marriage has traditionally entailed may cause the adolescent girl to feel an irrational antipathy towards her mother. The Glasgow School Welfare Officers—with whom I worked for a time—told me that this emotional condition was common in girls between the ages of thirteen and fourteen years, after which they calmed down. This is also the period of infatuation with rock 'n roll stars. It is not uncommon for girls of this age to run away from home and attach themselves to charismatic leaders of cults. Running away from home is the adolescent girl's favorite form of deviance. Whereas about six times as many boys as girls get involved in formal law breaking, running away is the only form of deviance which was found—in California, at least—to be more prevalent among girls—with the greatest frequency in the fourteen to fifteen year age group. With boys, running away is usually accompanied by breaking into places or other lawbreaking, but this applies to only a small proportion of the girl runaways.[2] In my experience, this instinctive *wanderlust* is much more prevalent in female than in male university students, and those who "get the bug" may be good scholars and well-adjusted young women.

MALADJUSTMENT-CONDUCIVE FAMILY SITUATIONS

Children can suffer deprivation—in the sense that they do not enjoy a secure attachment to a loyal and caring adult—even when living with their own parents. The family situations in which such deprivation can occur are described in the present chapter. They give rise, in the main, to similar forms of maladjustment, as reactions to such deprivation, that have been described in the chapters on children who have been separated from their parents. These types of maladjustment provide clues to the nature of the affectional breach between parent and child.

Children living in their own family may be exposed to one or more of four main sources of deprivation, each of which arises from typical patterns of defective parent-child relationships. The four sources of deprivation are as follows:

Source of Deprivation 1:

The child is under the threat of expulsion from the family.

Situation 1A occurs when *both* parents are harsh, unaffectionate and prone to expressions of rejection. A child's need for secure attachment to an adult can be satisfied by one parent only,[3] and, indeed, it is not uncommon for a child to look to either the mother or the father as the sole source of emotional support and affection and to be indifferent to or reject the other. Such a situation has obvious weaknesses—as will be seen when other sources of deprivation are discussed—but, provided the child remains with the preferred parent and the latter keeps in good health, the child is not emotionally deprived to the extent of becoming maladjusted. Probably most children establish preferences for one parent or the other, and this again causes no harm so long as the parents do not compete for the child's affection in a way that threatens their marriage.

It should be emphasized that it is rare for both parents to be unaffectionate to the point of giving the child the impression of being completely unloved and likely to be abandoned to other care. A child's maladjustment must therefore be attributed to such a situation only where there are objective indications of the parents' lack of concern and insensitivity.

Situation 1B occurs when the father wants the youngster out of the way as the "bad apple in the barrel" either because the child has always been a nuisance and a source of stress or for fear that the other children may be led astray. Typically, the child has been hard to raise because of some behavioral abnormality of congenital origin, which the parents see as being "born bad." More than one mother has described her son to me as "a nuisance from the day he was born." At the same time, the child's constitutional handicap of temperament may take the forms of anxiety proneness and an inability to withstand the ups-and-downs of family life.

Arthur was a whimpering, annoying baby and, as a toddler, used to wander off and get lost. Even at twelve years he was still a bedwetter and a headbanger, had a nervous tic, shouted in his sleep, and was scared of the doctor and dentist. His family was respectable and churchgoing, but the father was disgusted with the boy and feared he would have a bad effect on the other three children. In answer to his father's threats to have him "put away," the boy said openly that he did not care if this happened to him, and he even bragged to this effect in front of other boys. Moreover, he behaved in a way that was calculated to hasten his banishment. He stole from both parents, choosing, besides money, things that would cause inconvenience, and he finally took the money deposited in the gas meter. On the very day that he was charged with breaking into a house, he stole his father's new suit and his mother's electric iron and pawned them. These are classic symptoms of hostility. They might be described as a combination of an urge to escape from a loveless situation and a determination to kill his affection for his parents and any affection they might have left for him by restoring to the most provocative behavior.

Situation 1C is another of father-son antagonism. Typically, it originates when the husband and wife do not get along well, and the wife—partly to make up for what she lacks from her husband and partly to spite him—lavishes all her affection on her son. This naturally makes the father jealous of and antagonistic to the boy and, in extreme cases, determined to get him out of the family. The telltale signs of this type of family situation are a mother that criticizes the father openly, and a boy that condemns him bitterly as the source of the family troubles. Things become critical when the mother's nerves break, and she turns on her son, blaming him and giving way to the father's demand that he be removed.

Tom was in just such a position. When he was six his mother found it easier to give up on him when she had another child whom she could make the object of her affection. The father seized upon his bedwetting as an excuse for placing him in an institution for a period. Meanwhile, the father pressured the mother by threatening to desert her; and even after the boy's return home, he demanded repeatedly that Tom be sent away again. The latter's reaction was twofold: because of his loss of faith in his mother he became what she described as "very independent" in his affection for her, and he refused any endearments; he also stole money and other objects from both her and his father, and he ran away from home several times. He became depressed and was sometimes moody and surly. These were typical symptoms of the hostility reaction. At the same time, he had not overcome his anxiety for reacceptance. He was repentant for his wrongdoings, gave his mother presents, and wanted to help her in the home. The latter types of behavior are typical symptoms of anxiety about losing the mother. To compensate for his state of extreme deprivation, he lavished his affection on his younger brothers. At the same time, he looked forward to getting away from home by finding work on a farm. When children have been exposed to the stress of longstanding and nearly unbearable insecurity, they are apt to show signs of nervous exhaustion. Tom got very restless and irritable, complained of headaches, and said he was fed up with life. It is interesting to note that boys are much more likely than girls to fall into such states. The latter are usually temperamentally tougher and—as any member of the staff of a correctional school for girls will know—can go on being actively hostile much longer.

A similar threat of rejection *(Situation 1D)* may occur when an influential member of the family, other than a parent, brings pressure to bear to have the child removed. In the case of *Rose,* the antagonistic relative was a great-aunt who lived with the family. The father had deserted the family when the girl was three, and the mother, by her talk, admitted guardedly that her daughter got on her nerves. She said that she vacillated between defending her daughter against the great-aunt and joining the latter in rejection. At home, Rose did not steal from her mother but was surly and deceitful and very defiant when corrected. Children who feel rejected at home usually transfer their hostility to all the adults who have dealings with them. Rose turned the whole staff of her secondary school against her. The School Welfare Officer reported, "I cannot explain how bad things were at school; everyone heaved a sigh of relief when she left." She scored an 11 for Hostility on the Bristol Social Adjustment Guide (a score of 8 or more is rated as severe).

Situation 1E is created when well meaning parents threaten their child by saying that he or she will be sent away if bad behavior continues. They do so not because they have any intention of carrying out the threat but as a disciplinary measure. This kind of talk is probably not uncommon and, while it frightens the child, the response may be an improvement in behavior. Some children, on the other hand, are sensitive and prone to anxiety; they let the awful possibility of being sent away prey on their minds to the extent that they develop a counter-rejecting hostility. *Andrew* was like that. His family was an eminently stable one; his five sisters were described as outstanding, superior girls. But Andrew stole fruit and chickens from shops, broke into a church, and stole lead from church roofs. At home, he was moody, never smiled, set out to annoy, and had terrible temper tantrums during which he threw things. He would earn money doing jobs for other people, but he would not run errands for his mother. He skipped school and stayed away from home for hours. At school, he had a BSAG score of 7 for Hostility and a total score of 26 (20 was the criterion for maladjustment on the edition of the BSAG then in use).

In a stable family such as Andrew's, there must have been some special reason that made him feel so rejected that he reacted with this degree of hostility and other symptoms of maladjustment. The family had immigrated to Scotland from Malta when he was four; he said he hated the Maltese but liked the Scots. This uncalled for antipathy to people of his own kin offered a clue. It was suspected that the mother had been threatening to send him back to Malta if he did not behave better. When she was revisited she admitted that she had frequently done so. She agreed to stop the threats once it was explained to her that this was why her son was feeling rejected and that his bad behavior was his way of trying, in turn, to cut himself off from the family in order to soften the blow when he was sent away. From that day on, Andrew was "a different boy."

We have to ask why Andrew should have taken his mother's threats so seriously. It was not possible, in this case, to get a complete case history—including that of the pregnancy—which might have shown why he was so anxiety prone. It was known, however, that he had been a wanderer from a very early age, and that his mother had difficulty in keeping him in the house. This suggests that he was a temperamentally impaired child and therefore vulnerable to anxieties and uncertainties that would leave other children relatively unaffected.

The young age at which hostility can appear as a response to rejection supports the belief that this is one of the basic instinctive reactions of human nature. *Derek* was referred by his teacher to our Center for Educational Disabilities at the age of five. When the group of children he was in were asked to draw their families, he drew a crocodile. On being asked personally if he would like to draw his family, he replied, "Well, I'll draw my Irish dog." He did so, then said, "I'm going to kill him." Later he spontaneously drew himself, his father, and his brother, but he left out his mother.

Derek's father, a research scientist, and his mother told me of the asthma, bronchitis, and pneumonia which, from the age of 18 months, meant that he had to be constantly in and out of the hospital, although never for longer periods than ten days. His behavior problems started at the age of two and a half. Between two and a half and four he would get up in the night, take eggs out of the refrigerator, and drop them on the floor, or he would take a bite out of some food and then throw it in the garbage can. At the time I met the parents, Derek was getting up early and stuffing himself with cookies. He was also causing his mother anxiety and inconvenience by hiding in the home of one or the other of his friends; she had to go to the houses along the street to find him. He was quite unrepentant when found. "His mother," so reported the father, "gets into fighting matches with him. She has threatened to kill him."

At first the parents denied that they had threatened to have him sent away. However, the previous summer, when he was going into neighbours' garages and taking things such as tools and a fishing rod—which were naturally of no use to him—the parents threatened to have him put in jail. This did not stop him from stealing; it only further undermined his faith in them and provoked still more hostile acts.

Nevertheless, these symptoms of hostility in Derek were tempered by anxiety about his mother. In his affectionate moods he would put his arm round her and kiss her. He asked if he might do things around the house, and he set the table and vacuumed the bedrooms. The latter are symptoms of mother anxiety that will be discussed in subsequent cases in which the child fears being parted from the mother.

This case reveals how sincerely concerned and normally affectionate parents can—in moments of exasperation and bewilderment over their child's apparently willful bad behavior—utter threats which undermine their child's trust in them and in so doing make matters worse. After this had been explained to Derek's parents and they had desisted in their threats, the symptoms of hostility—his wanton destruction of food, his hiding, and his stealing from neighbours—ceased completely. When, some six years later, I met the father again, he told me that from that time on there had been no trouble, and Derek had settled down.

Source of Deprivation 2

The child loses the preferred or only parent and is left with an emotionally unsatisfactory substitute.

There are three typical situations in which this type of deprivation can occur. The first *(2A)* is when the parent whom the child has relied on for affection and a sense of permanence dies, and the child is left in the care of the other parent or another relative whom he finds it difficult to accept. This can happen when the surviving parent has been neglectful or harsh or has openly disapproved of the way in which the deceased parent has indulged the child. In the latter case, the non-preferred parent is looked upon as someone who denies the child the good things of life and is generally antagonistic—that is to say, in the child's eyes, unloving.

Neil's mother died of cancer when he was six. He had been, according to a neighbor, "the apple of her eye." After her death the father went out drinking every night, leaving his children unattended. Even before the age of eight—when he could be charged in court—Neil took to housebreaking, and he received his first conviction at the age of ten. The beatings he got from his father made him stay away from home.

When Neil was nine, his father remarried, but the boy refused to accept his stepmother, although she looked after him well and was a warm-hearted woman. Once, when she was putting him to bed, he asked to go to the toilet; half an hour later he was brought back by the police, who found him wandering in a public park. When he was twelve, while skipping school, the police caught him throwing bottles at passing cars. At this time, he was also charged with ill-treating a pigeon in the street. Such crazy, wanton behavior makes one suspect an avoidance compulsion. At the age of twelve, when he was asked if he ever thought of his mother, he screwed up his face as if some scary thought was crossing his mind and said, "There is too much to do; there's no time to think." It would be difficult to find clearer evidence of the mental process of avoiding a distressing memory. There must indeed be no chink in the consciousness of the victim of an avoidance compulsion through which a reminder of his anxiety can squeeze. Just what agonizing experiences of his mother's last illness were the subject of his trauma were not known. The care that he received from the stepmother must merely have acted as a reminder of them. When she was putting him to bed, the memory of his real mother must have welled up, and he had to flee from it. The screwing up of the face—sometimes as if the child is about to cry—when an interviewer touches on the subject of the avoidance was observed in several of the avoidance cases reported in *Delinquency and Human Nature*[4] (see especially that of Collins, p. 14).

The second of this group of situations *(2B)* differs from the first only in that the child loses contact with the loved parent owing to the breakup of the marriage. Because, in such cases, children normally stay with their mother, it is often the loss of the father as the preferred parent which sets off the child's behavioral breakdown. Several of these cases are described in *Delinquency and Human Nature* (e.g. Harris, p. 201, Knight p. 202). These boys usually reacted, like Neil, by getting into all kinds of irresponsible and delinquent activities as a means of escaping from their family problems. Marriage breakups also carry with them the danger that neither parent will want their teenage son, especially since the quarrels and threatened collapse of the family have made him unstable. In such cases, it is natural that the boy reacts by being hostile to the parent who he is convinced is trying to pass him on to the other (cf. Batchelor, p. 308; Howarth, p. 205; Hammond, p. 313).

The third situation threatening loss of the loved parent *(2C)* is where the child has come to regard a foster mother as his affectional mainstay and reacts to his separation from her as if from a true mother. The case of Ferguson, who was in this predicament—with his true mother threatening to claim him and finally succeeding in doing so—has already been described in Chapter 3.

Source of Deprivation 3

The mother is undependable as a source of affection and the father, even if available, offers no adequate alternative.

In situation *3A* the mother destroys the child's confidence in her because of her own emotional instability (which leads her to say the most cruel things), her harshness and insensitivity, or her depression. She threatens to harm the child, to desert the family, or to abandon the child to another's care.

The father may fail as an alternative source of affection for several reasons. He may be what in folk language is termed "not a family man." This means that he is uninterested in the children and leaves their disciplining to the mother, except when they cause him inconvenience. Alternatively, he may be an ineffective, chronic invalid or a drunkard who takes little or no part in the upbringing of the children and is not seen by them as a protective parent figure. Or he may be a stable type of man who, rather than face a difficult and neurotic wife, arranges his life so that he is seldom at home. He has a job that requires travelling or living away from home or some absorbing hobby which gives him an excuse for absenting himself during his free time. And of course, there is always the local bar.

Donald's mother had been reduced to a state of insensitivity, intolerance, and depression by her marital problems. Her husband was discharged from the army because of his health when the boy was eight, and he died of cancer when he was thirteen and a half. The parents quarrelled over the children, and the father was given to violence both against them and his wife. The mother openly rejected the boy, saying she could not put up with him any more. For his part, Donald became convinced that he was not wanted at home, and he said that he would like to get far away from it. He actually wanted to get sent to a correctional school, and there can be little doubt that this was the motivation for his delinquencies. It was only to be expected that, to make it easier to cut himself off from his family, he would resort to hostility, and the usual symptoms of this form of maladjustment were present. He stole food and money from his parents and from visitors. He was surly and defiant to his mother, and he was never in the house a minute more than necessary. Donald had passed the stage where he felt any anxiety about his mother's affection, telling the social worker openly that he wanted nothing to do with her any more.

In Situation *3B* the child is rejected by the mother in favor of her other children. It parallels *1B,* in which some constitutional behavior problem causes the father to regard a child as the bad apple of the family. The usual reason for the mother's rejection of one of her children is likewise some developmental impairment in the child, especially in the instinctive means of responding to maternal endearments or strange, irritating ways which she cannot undersand.

Even from his toddler days *Ross* never displayed as much affection to his mother as did his younger brother. The mother showed an open preference for the latter. She described Ross as self-willed, obstinate, and "unable to tell you his feelings." On the other hand, the father, in the mother's words, used to spoil him. Naturally, the boy became attached to the father and modelled himself on him. He gave little trouble and showed no signs of deprivation until the father went into the army. Within a few months he had found a substitute father in a milkman, and he skipped school in order to help him with his milk route. When, after some six weeks, he was discovered and forced to go to school, he helped the milk-man on Saturdays and Sundays, and he continued to do so for the re-maining four years that his father was away.

Ross, had, nevertheless, to live at home with his mother and endure her favoritism of his younger brother. His solution was to spend as little time as possible in the house. He said he "got bored sitting indoors." Asked if he had any hobbies, he said he was never home enough to do anything. When he left school and was making money, he went to the movies four or five times a week, and he took the neighbor's dog out—anything to remove himself from the constant reminder of his mother's lack of love.

An interesting feature of Ross's reaction to deprivation was that he dealt with it so far as possible within the bounds of acceptable behavior. After all, he still had a father who had shown him affection, even though he was away at the war.

Ross's undoing came from his conflict of emotions over his mother. He could not simply renounce any place in her affections. Indeed, he tried to win her over by buying her jewelry and flowers and other presents. However, his unconscious resentment towards her prevented him from being the dutiful son who gives his mother part of his wages. This he avoided by staying away from work. When his father returned from the war he took exception to this and promised the boy a beating. Continuing to evade work and having no money to bring home, Ross stayed out, sleeping in a stable. During the day he helped a fruit and vegetable seller, and then apparently lived with his family. Forced eventually to return home, he stole a bicycle and rode around on it until he was picked up, as if inviting arrest. With this and similar delinquencies he finally achieved his aim of securing his removal from the family. It was one of those cases in which a solution might have been found by the timely intervention of a social worker who could sum up the nature of the boy's insecurity.

In *Situation 3C* the child finds it difficult to accept his mother because he has formed an attachment to another woman who has taken her place in his affections. In such a situation, a child can get along with-out becoming maladjusted so long as the mother substitute is at hand and remains fond of him. It is on her loss—by her death, or the removal of one party or the other from the neighborhood—that the child signals his deprivation by maladjusted behavior. The mother substitute is often a grandmother, who lives in the same house or nearby, who has indulged the child or defended him against the mother's discipline. In other cases the child has formed a primary attachment to other adults who have looked after him for a period.

Source of Deprivation 4

The child fears the loss of the preferred or only parent.

In *Situation 4A* the child's anxiety arises from the mother's illnesses or childbirth difficulties, the latter especially if the mother's poor health originates from previous childbirths. Such anxieties lead to maladjusted behavior only when other circumstances combine to render them intolerable. One of these is the lack of a father with whom the child would feel happy and secure in the event of the mother's death. The other is a predisposition in the child to anxiety. This may be a matter of temperament, or the child may have been conditioned to apprehensions over the loss of the mother by early hospitalization or other separation. A mother who is always dwelling on her illnesses can also produce a state of chronic anxiety and conflict in her children. They resent having their lives centered around her supposed invalid needs; yet they cannot face up to their resentment because of their emotional dependence on her.

The characteristic type of behavior disturbance in this category is occasional lapses into irresponsible or delinquent activities in company with other children. *William's* mother had chronic stomach and kidney complaints; with six children and a husband without steady employment, she must have often become depressed and discouraged in a way that made her children anxious. At the age of ten years, William and his friends got caught in some petty stealing. His mother described him as wild, noisy, and restless at home.

Rowledge's mother had been ill for years with myxoedema and an abscess on her lungs for which she had been in hospital many times. He became especially worried about her when he learned that she was going to have another baby. Having kept out of trouble for the previous eighteen months, he appeared in court three times during the last three months of the pregnancy. He was committed to a correctional school the day after the baby was born.

Rowledge displayed the typical symptoms of avoidance excitement. He grew to detest school and skipped frequently. Of his jobs, he liked that of truck-deliverer's best because that afforded him a succession of physical sensations that could take his mind off his worries. Other types of work he found dull. He abandoned a youth club in favor of an amusements arcade in the city center, saying, "I used to think it was much more lively down there." It was "for fun" that he broke into shops and factories. He was one of those boys who, away from immediate reminders of his anxiety, was able to introspect about them. "When I went to bed," he told me, "I used to think the next morning that my mom might not be there. I used to think of other things and put it off." When at home, he had helped his mother with the housework, and he would hand her his pay envelope intact without even taking his own allowance. While she was in hospital he spent all of his salary on her. When his parents, on a visit to the correctional school, gave him some money, he spent it on roses for his mother.

All these boys—and others I knew who had similarly given way to compulsive avoidance behavior in order to escape from the anxiety of their mothers' illnesses—were temperamentally stable. No doubt they were more than usually sensitive and anxiety prone, but at school and in life in general they would have been seen as well-adjusted and likeable young people apart from their anxiety induced misbehavior. They illustrate the situational character of much behavior disturbance.

The source of the child's insecurity in *Situation 4B* is the parents' quarreling and one or both threatening to desert the home. To a child, the intention of a parent to abandon him or her by desertion is construed as disloyalty on a par with the threats of rejection which characterized the first source of deprivation. The child's reaction is, consequently, hostility. Combined with the hostility are avoidance symptoms arising from the dreaded thought of losing the mother; these symptoms are the usual mother anxiety behavior: helping with the housework and giving presents.

Roger's parents were at loggerheads, partly over money and partly because of the mother's surreptitious carrying on with a younger man. Both parents threatened to desert, and the father threatened suicide. In school, the boy showed extreme hostility, with thirteen indications on the BSAG. He was suspended from classes, and he became convinced that the entire staff was down on him, as no doubt they were. During his mother's illicit affair—when his father set him to watch her—he was convicted of housebreaking, for which a fine was imposed on his father. However, the boy paid this himself out of his earnings. He wanted to be sent away to a correctional school, but he did not want to go until after Christmas; he hoped his parents' quarreling would end by then.

Roger suffered from a number of habit disorders and neural impairments. He was subject to nervous mannerisms, was a bedwetter, and a restless sleeper. In recent years, he had blackouts and dizzy spells, such as are seen occasionally in children caught in an intensely distressing family situation. These constitutional weaknesses carried with them a likelihood of his being vulnerable to stress and prone to anxiety.

The third of those situations *(4C)* in which the child's anxieties originate with the fear of losing the parent arises from the threatened or actual breakup of the marriage—a situation likely to arise when the parent whom the child is living with and attached to proposes to remarry. Then these youngsters fear that they will not be wanted in the new relationship, and they may hear of or otherwise discover plans to dispose of them to the non-preferred parent or to a foster parent or institution (linking up with Situation 2B).

Owen's experiences of family life must have conditioned him to insecurity. His father—although reputed to be a thrifty man and steady in other respects—was imprisoned twice for successive bigamies, one result of which was that the boy was brought up by his grandmother. On her death—when he was eight—Owen was terribly upset, but he was looked after for about three years by some friends of the grandmother's. Only then did his mother take him into her own home. All went well until two years later when the mother set up house with another man with the intention of marrying him when her divorce came through. She then took Owen and his brother to his father and asked him to take them. The father eagerly agreed, but the woman he was living with refused. The scene was enacted in front of the two boys. Here was his mother—to whom he had grown exceedingly attached and who was his only effective parent—trying to palm him off onto a father he hardly knew and an antagonistic step-mother because of a stranger whom his mother proposed to marry.

From that day on Owen became exceedingly troublesome. He skipped school and stayed out late at night. When he left school, he mixed with gangs on the waterfront, and he did not come home until the early hours of the morning. He tired of every job after a short time, having over fifteen in three years. Finally, after a fight with the stepfather, he stole and smashed up a car.

The interesting feature of Owen's case was that he developed no hostility towards his mother. She gave a practical demonstration of her determination to keep him by refusing to enter a plea of "Beyond Control" against him on account of his delinquent behavior. He never lost heart in his struggle with the stepfather for his mother. Indeed, he won in the end because the mother left her second husband a few months later, taking her children with her.

WHAT VALUE IS THERE IN ANALYSING FAMILY SITUATIONS?

It must not be supposed that each of these four principal sources of deprivation—and the family situations which give rise to them—are self-contained in a way that one can always say of any maladjusted child, "The cause of that child's insecurity is such-and-such a maladjustment producing situation." In many cases this is indeed so, but in others a combination of two or more depriving situations can be discerned. The value of this analysis is that it provides the caseworker with possible reasons for a child's maladjusted behavior. In practical terms, it reveals the types of weaknesses to look for in the relationship of a maladjusted child and the parents. The type of the maladjustment acts as a signpost to the source of the child's deprivation. We have seen that where children are under a threat of expulsion from the family or feel otherwise rejected, they will counter with rejecting hostility. If the child fears the loss of the loved parent for a reason for which the parent cannot be blamed, and the youngster's anxiety is more than can be borne, escape from it will be sought through hectic distractions and excitements which become a compulsion dominating the child's whole life and appearing irrational and sometimes crazy.

These sources of deprivation also serve to remind us which are the fundamental deprivations causing maladjustment. They prevent us from attributing it to minor sources of emotional upset such as jealousy of brothers and sisters, feelings of inferiority, or poor self-image. Likewise, frustrations and discontents arising from lack of opportunity or having to put up with an unpleasant boss or teacher do not drive the emotionally stable young person to commit acts which are against his or her own best interests (and therefore, by our definition, maladjusted). When having to cope with someone in a position of authority who is unreasonable, the normal individual becomes very guarded so as not to provoke a clash. A situation is only critical, in the sense of provoking maladjustment, if it threatens the child's need for a place in the affections of a loyal parent figure.

chapter six

Treatment of the reactions to deprivation
Hostility and avoidance compulsion

People usually think of psychological treatment as taking place in a consulting room or center. With older children, personal counseling or other direct treatment by a therapist may sometimes be indicated, but the treatment described in this chapter consists mainly in removing sources of emotional stress from the child's life and offering the child rewarding personal relationships. It is carried out by those who are responsible for the youngster's daily care and education. Ideally, the strategy of this situational treatment is worked out by a psychiatrist or psychologist who has had experience with this method, but he or she should, in the main, work through parents, teachers, and the staff of residential schools.

Treatment should not be accorded the status of a mystique, as if the very intervention of the therapist is going to have some witchdoctorlike effect. The essence of treatment is understanding the nature and causes of the condition and communicating this understanding to those who have charge of the child. With such insight—and a willingness of all to follow its logic faithfully—the rest is a matter of genuine concern for the child and commonsense.

This does not mean that the course of treatment will always run easily and smoothly and bring quick results. The child's mentors may have to battle against the impressions made by previous emotional abuse. The child may try everyone's patience and, at times, make them indignant; the kindliest adults may be tempted to give such children up as a bad job and let them "get what they deserve."

THE HOSTILE CHILD IN SCHOOL

Indignation is indeed the natural reaction towards the behavior of the hostile child because it seems so senseless and wanton. As one teacher put it, "He waits until you are looking at him and then does something wrong." The motivation of the severely hostile child is to get on bad terms with adults and to make sure that the bad relationship continues. The child is sullen and does not answer or smile on being greeted. If a friendly hand is laid on the youngster's shoulder, it is shrugged off. The child does badly at work, as if trying to earn the teacher's disapproval. Rules are provocatively flouted as if to show rejection of human society. But when punished, the child is apt to react violently and with open hostility.

Naturally, these types of children bring a great deal of punishment on themselves, but it only makes things worse. The punishments reinforce their hostility—as proof that the strategy of making enemies of everyone is paying off. And they add to their conviction that the adult world is against them. With such children, teachers naturally find themselves in a quandary. Not to punish flagrant misbehavior would seem to undermine the basis of discipline, and other children might think it unfair if they are punished while the greatest transgressor gets off free. Teachers have to be persuaded that these are groundless fears. Only popular children are envied or imitated; the hostile child is anything but popular. The rest just think the child is stupid to run into so much trouble and get punished.

How then should a teacher deal with a hostile child who is openly defiant? The important thing is not to react by anger and antagonism. The only way to avoid doing so is to bear the child's emotional state in mind and to be aware of the goal of this hostility. One can then see every manifestation of it—surliness, stealing, running out of the classroom and hiding—as symptoms of the severity of the child's condition. In other words, the teacher has to cultivate the cool detachment of the therapist.

Nor need the teacher need feel that his or her professional competence is threatened by a failure to control the misbehaver. These children bring their hostility to school with them. Feeling rejected at home, they are resolved to cut themselves off from an affectional attachment that has proved unreliable. In order to be able to do this—and to kill their enduring need for love and security—they substitute hate. It is analogous, as stated earlier, to the fury of the lover spurned. Because of the intensity of their need for love, the substitutive hatred has to be all the more violent, and it becomes a compulsion which dominates their relations not only with the parents or other adults whom they see as rejecting them, but their relations with all adults. Naturally the teacher is among these. Indeed, the teacher who offers these hostile children open kindness may attract hostile reactions because kindness is a threat to them. It tempts them to begin to trust an adult again, and therefore has to be resisted.

Hostility has been described as an affection killing emotion. The term implies that, so long as the hostility has not given way to a fixed attitude of withdrawn enmity, the child's need for affection is still alive, as evidenced by the need to go on fighting it. Yet, if the adult does not respond to the hostility by a counterrejection, the child's assumption that everyone is an enemy is weakened. Very gradually, despite themselves, these children may move into a state of neutrality, and then begin guardedly to accept at least the companionship of the adult, provided the process is not rushed by offers of affection that are too open. The next stage, therefore—after having refrained from reacting to the child's misbehavior by anger—is to arrange that the child remain in contact with the teacher. Sending him or her out of the classroom only confirms the child's view that the teacher is just another rejecting adult. Physical presence tends to generate confidence and evoke feelings of belonging. If, for example, the child has run out of the class or out of the school building, the vice-principal or some other chosen mentor could arrange for the child to do lessons alone in the room with the adult. Reports of how hostages become friendly with their captors after a few days of living in close proximity to each other show the strength of the instinctive tendency to form bonds of fellowship among people who are merely thrown together. Occasionally, the mentor should say some necessary thing in a quiet, matter-of-fact tone, with no trace of sternness or sarcasm. After one or two such sessions, the mentor could send the child to deliver a message, and if the youngster carries it out faithfully, do so again. Care must be taken to avoid such statements as, "I'm glad you're doing better now." These may remind the child that he or she is forgetting the resolve to be antagonistic. After a few days, the child should be trusted to return to the classroom, while being allowed to sit in the mentor's room for half an hour or so each day to do homework or some other set task quietly. During these times, the mentor's concern should be demonstrated by giving the child a new pen or pencil, or a tissue to wipe a running nose.

It need hardly be said that punishment—especially of a corporal nature—will set back or completely nullify this process of gradually winning the child's confidence, since it places the teacher firmly in the camp of the rejectors. Punishment of the hostile child generates ever more hostile behavior, until, in the end, the youngster becomes uncontrollable and has to be removed.

Some children are in a betwixt-and-between stage of reverting to hostility when some incident or utterance reminds them of their rejection fears; at other times, when they feel more confident, they will seek to please and look for reassurances that they are wanted. In school, such children may respond to friendliness by demanding too much attention and trying to monopolize the teacher, only to revert to a bad—and some-times spiteful—mood when corrected or when their affection seeking is restrained. To tell these children to stop pestering will be construed as a rebuff, and it may prompt an act of stealing, spitefulness to another child, or making a mess of books. The teacher may have to tolerate the constant attention seeking for a while.

It should be emphasized that it is a mistake to always interpret attention seeking as a sign that the child lacks affection at home. It may be the spontaneous, uninhibited way in which certain children show their affection. If, moreover, these children have always been allowed to monopolize the adults at home in this way—as often happens with re-tarded children—they will naturally feel that they have the same right to their teacher's attention.

Since hostility originates with the child's lost confidence in his or her parents' loyalty and concern, all the teacher can do in school is to provide the child with a refuge from these anxieties and prevent the hostility from becoming generalized and turning into an antagonistic distrust of every-one. The teacher should not aim to take the place of the parent. Rather, it is a question of finding out, as soon as possible, why the child feels re-jected at home. In other words, someone has to make contact with the parents and, from what can be learned, form a hypothesis concerning the type of depriving situation which is generating the hostility (see Chapter 5). If no psychologist or social worker is immediately available to do this, a member of the school staff should visit the parents. The ideal person is a teacher acting in a pastoral capacity and allowed time to visit the homes.

HOSTILE CHILDREN AND THEIR PARENTS

The key to the treatment of hostile children is to discover why they have lost that sense of permanent belonging to a family with parents who care for them, such as most other children take for granted. Insight into their relations with their parents is best obtained by seeing the mother alone. If mother and father are interviewed together they will almost certainly cover up their differences and put on a defensive front about their treatment of the child. One modern approach to family therapy is for the counselor to hold a discussion with the entire family. But this mode of treatment is more suited to the settlement of parent-adolescent struggles, when it is a matter of reaching agreement about respective rights, liberties, and responsibilities of parents and children based on a reasonable plan for living together. It is not so much an exploration of the reasons for a child's maladjustment as a negotiation toward a contract. It would not do to have a maladjusted child present while interviewing the mother. She would feel awkward, and would almost certainly want to send the child away to play so she could speak freely.

Preferably, the mother should be seen in her own home. There she will be in her own territory, whereas she may feel intensely uncomfortable if interviewed in an office. Women from traditional cultures who have had little experience of meeting professional people are apt to be overawed. All one may get from them is "Yes sir" or "No sir;" if they give a wrong answer they are afraid to correct it. I have also found that mothers can recall more when at ease in their own homes.

The strategy for the treatment of hostile children depends on the extent to which the parents are willing to cooperate with the social worker in removing the causes of insecurity. One cannot judge the parents by first impressions. One or both of them may be in a state of apparently unrelenting antagonism, but the fact that someone else is concerned about the child may reawaken parental feelings.

PARENTAL INTOLERANCE
INDUCED BY STRESS

In judging the attitudes of parents, it is important to bear in mind that one may be meeting them at a time of family crisis or other acute stress. In an extremely stressful situation to which no rational solution can be found, even otherwise stable people deal with the situation in an immediate way without thinking about further consequences. It is indeed a natural instinctive provision for escaping from danger. It is seen in the panic of people in a building on fire or on a sinking ship. In such circumstances, an emergency system of reactions comes into play which is quite different from the individual's normal behavior. In everyday life, one sees lesser manifestations of this stress reaction when people get irritated or lose their tempers. They are then apt to do and say things which do not correspond with their normal feelings. When people have been exposed to longstanding stresses which become too much for them, they may revert to a state which—for want of a more elegant term—I have called "irritable-depressive-nontolerance." It is a combination of anger and depression.

Mothers sometimes get into this state when assailed by the multiple stresses of marital discord, lack of a husband to provide for the family and to share in the control of the children, chronic illness, and the strain of having a maladjusted and delinquent child. Her reaction is to attack the most immediate source of stress, namely the child. From loving, she turns to hating; saying she cannot stand the child around her any more, even threatening murder if he or she is not taken away. It is also in this state that parents attack their children physically. Their cruel treatment of the child—whether it be by words or actions—is quite out of keeping with their love up to the point that the stress condition overcomes them.

Subsequently, when the parents have recovered, they regret their temporary rejection of the child; but by then the damage has been done. The child has heard the mother saying that she wants to get rid of him or her, and, moreover, she has said it vehemently and in no uncertain terms— as if she meant it, which, at the time, she did. With faith in her thus shattered, the child's natural reaction is to look elsewhere for a more loving parent. This means stifling affection for the mother, which the child tries to do by running away and becoming independent of her, and stealing from her. This is the reaction of hostility with its motivation of killing affection.

When parents get into this irritable, depressive state they may react with antagonism against the social worker or the representative of the school. One has to listen patiently—agreeing and sympathizing where possible—and, at the first opportunity, get them on your side by deflecting the conversation on to the hardships and injustices they have suffered. Perhaps, also, a way can be found of alleviating their material difficulties or settling their quarrel with local officials.

It may be necessary to arrange for the child who is the focus of this irritable, depressive antagonism to be removed temporarily to other care. However, it is of the utmost importance that neither parent be allowed to enter a plea of "Beyond control" against the child. The ritual of being formally abandoned by the parent is a trauma which, in my experience, nearly always prevents the child from accepting the parent again. Arrangements for the removal of children should never be discussed in their presence, for this can have the same effect of permanently destroying their faith in their parents. The child's temporary removal from home allows time for the parents' love for the child to come to the fore again. Whether this will happen will be discovered only in the course of time. As seen in Chapter 4, the healing of the estrangement between parent and child may take up to two years.

Parents may utter threats of sending children away in moods of temporary irritation, or even as a means of discipline. They do so with no sense of the effect it has on the child. Children tend to take everything adults say literally because with their lack of experience of life; they do not realize how people can say things without meaning them. A woman teacher once gave me a good illustration of this: when her two young sons were being more than usually boisterous, she told them that she was going to change them for two nice quiet little girls. About three weeks later one of them asked her, "Mommy, are you still going to change us for two little girls?" Many mothers, when their family gets on their nerves, threaten to leave to see how they manage without her. Most threats of this kind do little harm because the children do not take them seriously or soon forget about them. On the other hand, some children are constitutionally sensitive and prone to anxiety, and they let the threat prey on their minds. They become convinced that the parent intends to send them away or desert the family, as the case may be. The possible reasons for this varying vulnerability of children to deprivation are discussed in Chapter 9.

If you ask a parent bluntly if he or she has been making threats to desert or send the child away, you will probably get a denial. The interviewer can use a reminiscing technique about other parents and children: "Some parents, when they are fed up, threaten their child that he or she will be sent away if the bad behavior doesn't stop, and the child takes it to heart." Being told that other parents say such things induces the parents to drop their defensiveness and admit that they have often made such threats. Mothers and fathers should then be reminded how implicitly children believe their parents. The fears that easily uttered threats give rise to, and the reactions they produce, should then be explained: children have to have complete trust in their parents; if this trust is shaken, they may well try to cut themselves off from them for good; their way of doing this is to be really bad, stealing from the parents and so on.

THE TECHNIQUE OF THE INTERVIEW

A good way to start an interview—after the usual courtesies are over—is to express interest in the child's progress and then remark, "but your child seems to be upset about something." Then ask the parent to talk about the child's early life: what illnesses the child has had, what kind of a birth, the progress as a baby, age of walking and talking, and so on. These questions should lead to the child's temperament when very young and at the present time, the manner of play with other children, and finally, the child's behavior at home and whom he or she is most fond of. This approach relieves the parent of the apprehension of being taken to task for the child's bad behavior in school. It also enlivens memories of earlier and possibly happier times with the child. In the latter part of the interview, the mother will probably be prepared to discuss her relations with her husband and their respective attitudes to the child.

Again, direct questions should not be asked on delicate matters, but should be of a nature that the mother is willing and pleased to answer: Can you think of anything in your child's life that is worrying him?; Does she get along well with her Dad? How does he spend his free time; With whom does he spend it with? Does she like to spend her free days with a grandparent or some other adult? Is he always out with the boys down the street?—If so, have they been getting into mischief? For those who intend to make a serious study of family casework, there are forms available that list the information to be sought and interpret it.[1]

It is important to note that the preceding questions use the language with which people traditionally speak about emotions, attitudes, and personal relationships. The college student, reared on psychological phraseology, may have to make an effort to learn this language. It is advisable to take notes during the interview, unless the mother is suspicious of the social worker—but in these cases one is usually kept standing at the front door. Contrary to what might be thought, taking notes does not make the mother nervous or cautious about what she says. The effect is just the opposite: it impresses upon her that what she is telling you is important. She will feel gratified and flattered, because it will probably be the first time that a professional person has given her the opportunity to speak freely and at length. Consequently, she will be careful to give a full and accurate account. More than once, a mother has sent me a letter the next day correcting something that she told me. In the note taking, the actual phrases used by the mother should be recorded as well as dates and events. The pauses which are necessary to get it all down are valuable; the moments of silence give the mother time to recollect and to summon the courage to reveal hidden facts. Although caseworkers may have a list of the essential information required in front of them or in their mind, it should not be followed in a way that breaks the mother's spontaneous account. The notes taken can later be coded and written up in a logical sequence.

The working over of the information which this writing up involves provides a procedure for thinking about a case. The evidence should be pieced together and compared with the various standard situations liable to produce maladjustment (described in Chapter 5). Probably no one piece will be an exact fit, but the caseworker will be able to recognize a source of deprivation similar to one of the standard situations. There may be a double source of deprivation, a combination of two maladjustment producing situations.

COUNSELING THE PARENTS
OF THE HOSTILE CHILD

It remains to be considered what advice the caseworker should give to the parents once he or she feels confident that the source of the child's anxiety has been located. This interview should be arranged when the father can also be present. The therapeutic value of an objective discussion can then be extended to both parents. It gives them an opportunity to review their feelings towards the child and to overcome any antagonistic or rejecting impulses they may have had. Such moods will persist only so long as the parents feel defeated, because they have tried everything they know and it has made the child worse. During the interview they can be given insight into the reasons for the child's hostile behavior by using the techniques suggested formerly, and led to see that the hostility is an expression of the child's fear of being separated from them. They should then be counselled that however angry they get, they must never threaten to have their child sent away, nor even to make remaining in the home conditional upon good behavior. Nor must either of them, in a mood of disheartenment, threaten to desert the family. If such threats are made during quarrels between themselves, they must try to contain their anger in front of the children. This may be utopian advice, but at least during a quarrel the mother should refrain from the threat to leave or to play act it by packing her bag and ostentatiously leaving by the front door, only to creep in later at the back door when the children are in bed.

The parents should not be advised to overlook the child's bad behavior, since they cannot be expected to adopt the thoroughgoing objectivity of the professional therapist. They need some positive substitute for the beatings and threats to throw the child out of the home that are their usual method of dealing with running away or stealing. In place of the threat to get rid of the child, the parents should express their anger and disapproval in words that emphasize their determination to keep the youngster: "You're my son, and I'm going to see that you grow up to be a decent young man"; "You're our own flesh and blood, and we're going to stick by you, but it's up to you to behave as if you're our daughter and not shame us before other people."

It will often be found that when the threats of sending away or deserting—and of course murder, if such were made—are discontinued, the stealing and running away will also cease. The parents should, however, be forewarned of an occasional recurrence—in the form of an isolated act—to test the genuineness of their affection. If the father threatens that the next time he will tell the judge to put the youngster away, then, sure enough, there will be a next time. If a child, over some years, has become deeply distrusting of a parent's interest, he or she may well put the new concern that the parent shows to the test, and the test is likely to be a very severe one that invites renewed rejection.

A lapse by the child which results in a court appearance should be used by the parents as an opportunity to demonstrate that they are determined to keep the child. They should express this determination in no uncertain terms before the judge or juvenile panel. By doing so, they will have passed the loyalty test and avoided the disloyalty trap that the child has set for them (Other examples of the tactic of positive reassurance were given in Chapter 4). If the parents bear the principle of it in mind, there will be innumerable ways of demonstrating their intention that the child will share their home until age permits a normal departure.

THE AVOIDANCE-DOMINATED CHILD

A great deal of what has been said about the counselling of the parents of the hostile child applies to the case of the child whose behavior is dominated by an avoidance compulsion. It is a question of first discovering the source of the child's anxiety. This will be a situation in which the child fears losing the parent to whom he or she looks for care and support, but does not feel that the rejection is deliberate. When a mother makes threats of deserting the family in a harsh and angry mood, these threats are likely to be perceived as evidence of her willingness to abandon her family; the reaction will be one of hostility. Where, on the other hand, the mother's threats to leave the family spring from a state of desperation resulting from quarrels with the father, the child will blame the latter and not the mother. The child's likely reactions will be to do her domestic chores in order to make life more tolerable for her, while at the same time seeking distractions as a way of forgetting the worry. In some cases, the child is afraid to leave the mother's presence. In other cases, the search for excitement and wild company keeps the child away from home. One of the most common sources of anxiety is about the mother's health. It may provoke a temporary phase of distraction seeking misbehavior. As with the hostile child, the possible sources of anxiety should be reviewed until the evidence points to one of the deprivation situations described in the previous chapter.

It was mentioned in Chapter 3 that the subject of the avoidance is a particular episode or a recurrent traumatic scene. Usually this is directly related to the source of the child's anxiety. A mother may go to pieces emotionally after another of her children has been killed in a street accident (I know of a case in which this happened outside the family home). The child dates the onset of problems from that day and cannot bear the constant reminders of the catastrophe. Youngsters may try to blot out the memory of the death of a loved grandmother to whom they had looked as their primary source of affection.

It may not be possible—at any rate, in the first interview—to bring the traumatic episode or nagging reminder of the child's anxiety to light. However, at the second interview, with the father also present, it can be explained that the unruly behavior may really be an effort to forget something that is causing the child distress. This will, in turn, comfort parents who are completely at a loss to understand why their son or daughter has suddenly turned into a truant, a ne'er-do-well, and possibly a thief. As they join in trying to get at the source of the child's avoided worry, they will be equipped with a positive alternative of action which forestalls desperate panic measures on their part.

Children who are using these means of avoiding their anxieties are never able to reveal their source. It is useless to ask the natural question, "What's bugging you?" or "Why do you do it?" If the child mentions that it is the mother's health, one can be sure that it is something else—possibly the fear that she will desert the home. Children may account for their restless behavior by saying that it was just for fun, that they are bored, or that they dislike their neighborhood. They may give another hint of their avoidance compulsion by saying that they cannot stand being shut in and have to get into the open air, whatever the weather. Normal children don't dislike the surroundings in which they are brought up, however drab they may be. Children under an avoidance compulsion insist on being out of the house, or school, even if they have nowhere to go. They embark upon any mischief that presents itself and join with other children bent on similar pursuits.

When avoidance driven children are given to deviant or grossly abnormal behavior, it is best that they be removed temporarily to residential care, away from the needling reminder of their insecure domestic situation. There they will probably settle down to normal, sensible behavior. The danger is that on their return home the old problem and its associations may once more drive them to seek forgetfulness in restless unruliness. This serves to underline the importance of working in the meantime with the parents to discover the source of the child's anxiety.

To immediately attempt a direct defusing of the avoidance compulsion by confronting children with the episode or situation that they are trying to block out of their minds may have adverse consequences; it is best to wait until they have been away from home a few months and their family problems have lost their urgency. Even then, the avoidance will be found to be surprisingly strong. When the avoided event is discussed with the child, he or she will typically murmur answers in a dreamy, absent-minded state—immediately after—the child will still profess no memory of it. At this stage, the effort to bring the memory into consciousness has never, in my experience, had any undesirable consequences; along with the removal of the objective reasons for the anxiety, the confrontation may strengthen the child sufficiently to enable him or her to live at home again.[2] Much more research is needed, however, before it can be said to what extent such defusing procedures are necessary to free the young person from the compulsion.

chapter seven

Handicaps
of temperament
Unforthcomingness
and overdependence

INNATE DIFFERENCES
OF TEMPERAMENT

When Elsa, the lioness that Joy Adamson[1] reared, led her cubs across a stream, two of them swam after her, but the third remained on the bank crying pitifully. Since the cubs were not long born and it is hardly conceivable that the mother treated them differently in any significant way, we have to suppose that the third cub suffered from a constitutional timidity. Anyone who has had contact with domestic animals—whether they be cattle or dogs or cats—is well aware of individual differences in temperament among them, which, considering the standard conditions in which they are raised, must be inborn. The same applies to human babies: some are placid, others fretful, some venturesome, others timid. As with Elsa's cubs, these personality differences seem to persist through childhood until puberty. Hutt and Bhavnani[2] found that preschool children rated as "inventive explorers" in their play with a novelty box were, after an interval of four to five years, between two and three times more creative than those who at the preschool level had been "non-explorers." The preschool non-explorers who were boys were also found by their primary teachers to be "non-curious," while the girls were "sensitive and easily discouraged."

EFFECTIVENESS-MOTIVATION

The above authors were dealing with one of the most significant components of temperament in human beings and indeed in the higher animals. White[3] called it the urge to competence. From a study of the infant behavior of my son which did not seem to be directed to the satisfaction of any physical need, I concluded that there must be some independent urge toward effectiveness as such,[4] which closely parallels White's concept of competence. I recorded how my son, even from the age of two and a half months, liked to create noise by knocking a rattle. A little later, he showed great glee at a peek-a-boo game, indicating a pleasure in anticipation and recognition. At five and a half months, he experimented in making strange noises through his mouth. At one year, he insisted on feeding himself, although he got much less food this way than when fed by an adult. He alarmed his parents by standing in his high chair and rocking it. At fourteen months, he had a craze for filling receptacles, fitting lids on pans, and opening and shutting drawers (not being deterred even when he caught his fingers). At fifteen months he evinced great delight in recognizing pictures of people and animals. Once he had learned to walk (itself a most satisfying achievement), he liked to lift a heavy object such as a hammer, or to push his buggy around. He explored by twisting the knobs of the radio, trying to write with a stick, and pushing hairpins into the electric power sockets. All these spontaneous activities—whether they consisted of producing a noise or other notable effect, achieving a goal, learning about his world by recognizing objects and experimenting—amounted to a heightening of his competence or effectiveness. The strength of such motivation varies greatly from child to child. Each extreme can become a handicap.

UNFORTHCOMINGNESS—A DEFICIT
OF MOTIVATION

All children have natural fears—of strange objects, strange people, of committing themselves to a task at which they may fail, (that is to say, at which they would be ineffective). A normal infant beginning a new activity is so cautious that it is hard to decide whether the result is intended or not. Once, however, children see that they can master an activity, they throw themselves into it with zest. Children with a normal level of effectiveness motivation feel a challenge to master their fears. Murphy[5] gives some wonderful examples of the determination of a little girl of just over two to conquer her fears of thunder and low flying planes. By the age of four and a half, she had succeeded to the extent that she could comfort her younger brother.

Children with a low level of effectiveness-motivation remain dominated by their fears. They shrink from anything strange, freeze when confronted with a problem—even though it is within their ability to solve—and show no curiosity or venturesomeness. The result is that they get to know little about their world, they acquire few skills in solving problems, and their concept development remains at a low level. I met so many children like this in the course of my work with slow learners that I came to see "unforthcomingness," as I termed it, as a frequent cause of learning failure. It had not been recognized as such because the children in question are regarded as dull or retarded, as indeed they are as far as their functioning is concerned. But the reason for their backwardness is a deficit of motivation rather than of intelligence. In their home surroundings—where they deal with familiar objects and cope with well practiced tasks—they are sensible and competent even though still unventuresome.

Unforthcomingness is one of the underreacting, inhibited forms of maladjustment which are sometimes grouped under the catch all term of "neurotic behavior." However, its resemblance to other types of inhibited behavior is only superficial. If we do not make a distinction between unforthcomingness and overdependence, depression or withdrawal, we shall lack the understanding of the child's problem necessary for choosing the correct form of treatment. While it is true that persistent unforthcomingness is undoubtedly congenital in origin, depression is usually the outcome of chronic infections or long exposure to emotional stress. Emotionally withdrawn children are those who have become so discouraged from being deprived of loving attachment to an adult that they shrink from getting involved in any further human attachments. Unforthcoming children, on the other hand, are very affectionate to those adults who win their confidence. Their behavior has much in common with the behavior of the overdependent children described later, but the latter's handicap consists in the use of strategies to remain under the mother's wing rather than lack of confidence.

Adrian showed how the typical unforthcoming child copes with life, and how his behavioral handicap resulted in backwardness. He was brought by his parents to our Center for Educational Disabilities at Guelph when he was just over eight because he wasn't making progress in a special class. At this age, he had no reading ability and could not even recognize all the numerals up to ten.

The teacher described him as a child who was afraid of committing himself to solving problems. His modes of evasion were making random guesses when he could have got the solution with a little thought, and seeking distractions. He had little ambition to succeed, and he was very afraid of failure. With an IQ of 85 it would have been easy to conclude that he was just a dull child, but the teacher also noted that, while not interested in regular learning activities, he talked intelligently and found his own interests.

When Adrian was introduced to learning games which had been designed to correct faulty attitudes such as his lack of confidence, he used the strategies he had developed—in common with many other unforthcoming children—in order to avoid having to commit himself. He would make as if to choose a card (bearing the right letter for the initial sound of a word) meanwhile waiting for a sign from the teacher indicating that his choice was correct. If no such confirmation was received, he would try another card. In this way he got the adult to make every decision for him. In fact, he nearly always made the right choice the first time but did not trust himself. His mother said he was just the same at home. If asked to do a simple job he would say, "I can't do it, it's too hard for me." There was a real danger that he would retreat into a state of virtual retardation.

However, when given a hint about how to solve a problem, Adrian went to do it successfully. Within six weeks he had become much more relaxed and assertive. After another two weeks, he was even more outgoing and sure of himself. He no longer looked to the teacher for confirmation of his responses, and he showed great glee at winning a game. It would have been too much to expect that he could completely overcome his constitutional lack of confidence in so short a time; with a new teacher he reverted to his ruse of trying to read an adult's face rather than think out an answer for himself. But he made steady progress and enjoyed success. He had discovered that there was fun to be had in coping with life, and his retreat into retardation had been halted.

TEMPERAMENTAL UNFORTHCOMINGNESS AND NORMAL CAUTION

We have to consider to what extent we are justified in describing Adrian's lack of confidence as a handicap of temperament, which implies—barring some postnatal brain injury—that it was innate or congenital. Not all children who show this trait are temperamentally handicapped. Most young children are unforthcoming on first finding themselves in a strange situation, but once they have reassured themselves they open up. People of all ages shy off from a difficult problem or even one which contains an element of trickiness or uncertainty. There is a point at which the ordinary person will give up trying to work out a problem and make a random guess. It is not that the avoidance strategies of the unforthcoming child are by their nature abnormal, but that children of this type use them as their chief means of coping with life. They are content to be ineffective. Such habitual unforthcomingness is quite different from the shyness and caution of the normal child.

Our schools for the retarded contain many of these unforthcoming children who have settled down to a life of non-accomplishment. They have duly acquired low IQs because the tasks of a mental test are designed to be unfamiliar and to require thinking out; they present just the sort of problem at which the unforthcoming child balks. Because they never bring their abilities into use, no one can tell what abilities they may have. There is nothing to indicate that they are innately retarded; rather, they become so from a failure to develop mental competence, as do normal children, by responding to the challenges of learning and problem solving.

THE ISSUE OF CONGENITALITY

Congenitality means that the condition originates at or before birth. The reaction of many goodhearted people is that to admit this amounts to the condemnation of a child to permanent handicap. This is not necessarily the case. Many congenital conditions can be successfully treated, or the affected children grow out of them. In a program designed to give Adrian the confidence to solve problems on his own, he improved steadily. At puberty, many unforthcoming boys suddenly become transformed into outgoing, assertive youths. We need not feel that we have to deny the congenitality of a form of behavior disturbance for humanitarian reasons. Indeed, it may be more unkind to always insist that it must be acquired after birth, since this implies—probably quite unjustly—that the mother or whoever brought up the child is to blame. It is, in short, important both for human and therapeutic reasons to recognize that a condition may be congenital.

There are two yardsticks by which the probability of the congenital origin of a handicap can be gauged. The first is its appearance very early in life, before the child is exposed to environmental influences which could have brought on the condition. Lois Murphy[5] devoted much thought and observation to temperamental differences in children. She noted (p. 343) that most of those children who had been of average or above average activity level as infants continued to deal with the environment in active ways. The trait she called autonomy—children taking responsibility for how they coped with the world rather than allowing themselves to be directed by others—tended to remain constant from infancy through the pre-school years.*

The second yardstick is the presence of other types of impairment. Whichever prenatal or natal factors produce impairment tend to produce more than one. Consequently, if a child has one handicap, there will be a greater than average chance that he or she will have another of quite a different order. If a child has two distinct impairments, the chances are even greater that there will be a third, and so on, leading to what has been

*Murphy's concept of autonomy forestalled Rotter's concept of internal control, i.e. making the running oneself, as opposed to external control—being run by other people. Both are facets of effectiveness-motivation.

called the *multiple impairment syndrome*.[9],[10] Consequently, we may expect to find a range of physical and neurological defects alongside a congenital handicap of temperament.

In Adrian's case, his mother said he had been inactive in the womb compared with her two older children, and he had periods of ominous stillness. By the time he was five to six weeks old she was sure there was something wrong with him because he was so limp when she held him. She complained to the doctor that he was "too good." He did not sit up alone until he was fourteen months, nor walk until eighteen months. Already in his attempts to walk she noticed his unwillingness to risk failure. He would not try anything if it appeared unsafe. He did not get into things or pull things apart, nor was he noisy and assertive as her other boy had been. He was given blocks to play with quite early, but he took much longer than her other children to get to the stage of building with them. Yet he was content and not in the least frustrated. In short, his coping style of avoiding challenge and commitment—which is the central characteristic of unforthcomingness—had been present from infancy. Moreover, he was a typical example of the multiple impairment syndrome. He was slow to learn to speak, using single words only until nearly five, and at the age of nine he still had a slight speech defect. His mother also remarked on his poor coordination at this age: he did not run like other boys, he was beginning to catch, but not like a normal nine-year-old—"You couldn't send him out to play baseball."

If, as would appear, Adrian's handicap of temperament was congenital, what was the cause of it? Lois Murphy had also wondered why the little boy Steve (p. 232) was so quiet, undemanding, and sensitive (that is, unforthcoming), in contrast to his robust sister. She could find no significant differences in the way they were treated; the mother was consistently permissive with all her children. But during the pregnancy the mother had been worried about the possible loss of her own mother, who was ill in the hospital. In my own studies of the prenatal determinants of handicap,[11],[12] a pregnant woman's anxiety over the serious illness and possible death of her own mother was one of the stresses related to physical and behavioral impairments in the child, and among retarded children unforthcomingness as such was found to be related to pregnancy stress.[13]

It was curious that Adrian's mother gave me a very similar report of her own pregnancy. Her mother had had Parkinson's disease for years, was constantly in and out of the hospital because of her psychiatric state, and was difficult to handle. At the time of this pregnancy she was being particularly difficult. Moreover, the mother's father was also ill at the time, and he died six months after Adrian was born. It was, of course, coincidental that the mothers of both Steve and Adrian should report emotional stresses from the same cause during the pregnancies preceding the births of their unforthcoming children. In the above studies of prenatal stresses, the most damaging types of emotional stress were those arising from marital discord and other ongoing negative personal relationships. In a stable, thriving family with good neighborly relations, such interpersonal stresses would be rare, but the one source of stress that cannot be eliminated in the stable family is the poor health and feared death of loved ones. This possible cause of unforthcomingness and other handicaps of temperament occurring in stable families needs to be further studied.

THE TREATMENT
OF UNFORTHCOMINGNESS

The guiding consideration—which must always be uppermost in the mind of the teacher or therapist in the treatment of unforthcoming children—is that they should never be pushed beyond the limits of their confidence. If they are presented with a task that they *perceive* as too hard—whether it is or not—they will resort to one of their strategies of avoidance. Owing to their apprehensive temperament, these strategies will never be in the form of *active* distractions, as in the case of the overreacting child. Usually, they will avoid thinking out an answer by making a hesitant, tentative guess, or by not responding at all. It is easy then to assume—with our predilection for ideas about level of intelligence—that they cannot manage the task. In truth, they have not attempted it. If—on the assumption of their being dull or retarded—no further attempts are made to stimulate their mental development, they are helped on their way to retardation.

To make sure that this tendency to retreat is not activated, the tasks presented to unforthcoming children should be objectively too easy. They should be such that these children can see the answer before they have time to worry about the awful prospect of failure. So far as possible, the children should be allowed the experience of uninterrupted success, so that they become conditioned to an expectation of "I can do it." The task should never be presented as if it were an item in a test ("See if you can do this one," and so on). For this reason it is better to work with a pair of children, one of whom is not unforthcoming. The teacher can then give each of them a very simple task: joining the half pictures of the Two-Piece Puzzles which form the first item of the Flying Start Kit. In this way, the moment of tension during which the teacher waits for the child to make a move can be avoided. The unforthcoming child will probably wait to see what the other child does, but this is all to the good. In this interval, the child is deciding whether he or she can do the same. The teacher should even ignore a lack of response and give the other child another puzzle to complete. The unforthcoming child will learn by observation and respond in his or her own time—when confidence in managing the task has come.

The treatment of the unforthcoming child needs considerable self-discipline on the part of the teacher. One has to resist the temptation to say things like, "Come on, I know you can do that; you did it yesterday." Any goading is the signal for the child's retreat into a pose of incompetence. When working with children of this type who are thought to be retarded the unsuspected ability that they reveal may so excite the teacher that harder tasks are given to see if they can manage these also. The result is a setback in the slow progress of their conditioning in confidence. Each time these children are confronted with a task for which they are unprepared, their former apprehensions are revived. When a child has succeeded he or she should be given repetitions of the same task until a willingness is shown to move to the next stage. When the child has completed the Two-Piece Puzzles easily and confidently, an opportunity should be given for observing other children doing the Four-Piece Puzzles; after awhile, one of the puzzles should be left, perhaps half done, for the child to complete if he or she cares to do so.

The learning of the basic subjects should also be in groups, where unforthcoming children—after the period of observation which is so necessary for them—can join in when ready. On no account should they be called upon to answer. This sounds like a very slow process, but the usual method of question-and-answer teaching will cause the unforthcoming child to "return to the shell" again (to use the phrase by which teachers often describe this refusal of any challenge). In effect, once these children have gained confidence, their very caution causes them to attend closely in order to be sure of being right when they do commit themselves. Consequently, unforthcoming children can develop a very good learning style and surpass those who are inclined to respond without forethought.

When, owing to circumstances, individual work with the unforthcoming child is necessary, the tutor has to be prepared to wait for the child to make up his or her mind when ready, meanwhile being careful not to give any hint to the answers by word, facial expression, or gesture. Adrian's knack of getting his teacher to tell him all the answers is a standard strategy of unforthcoming children which teachers continually reinforce. The child then becomes like the circus horse that can "count" by picking up a cue from its trainer. So long as these children succeed in getting other people to find solutions for them, they will never learn to use their own minds.

One of the reasons why it pays to continue working patiently with unforthcoming children—even though progress is slow—is that during adolescence, and sometimes quite suddenly at puberty, their habitual apprehensiveness may be replaced by normal confidence and even assertiveness. I recall one such boy who in his teens became a keen motorcyclist. Another boy, who had been described in teachers' reports on him year after year as "too timid to learn," acquired so much self-confidence within a short time after leaving school that he volunteered to perform card tricks before an audience in his youth club, and he did so with the skill and aplomb of a practiced conjuror. But owing to their unforthcomingness during their school days and the lack of any remedial program suited to their handicap, both these young fellows were completely illiterate. It helps if the unforthcoming child achieves even a partial literacy to build on in later years.

OVERDEPENDENCE

The coping strategies of the overdependent child are superficially similar to those of the unforthcoming. She (they are mostly girls) refuses to attempt tasks; but whereas the unforthcoming child wants to please and therefore, except in the most extreme cases, makes some attempt, the overdependent child refuses in an absolute manner.

When five-year-old *Betty* was asked to do the Two-Piece Puzzles of the Flying Start Learning-to-Learn program, she said, "I'm not going to." But when the pieces were put in front of her she did them without hesitation. Even with the Four-Piece Puzzles there was no timorous, random placing or trying to pick up clues from the adult. Both her initial refusal and the confidence with which she performed the task are quite untypical of the unforthcoming child. Her response was with the Mailboxes: at first she did not want to check the other player's postings by matching up the halves of the pictures, but when she tried, she found she got great enjoyment out of doing so; she went on to do the posting, which involved decision making. Apart from her stubbornness, she would make mistakes on purpose when she felt like doing so. Her teacher reported, "I feel, at times, that she knows but is playing a sort of game with me."

The overdependent differs also from the unforthcoming child by her sudden switches of attitude. Having decided that she liked the learning games, Betty threw herself into them with enthusiasm. The teacher noted in her log, "Laughing, happy, willing to talk. What a change!" No temperamentally unforthcoming child could let herself go like that.

Nevertheless, when her mother or younger sister appeared, Betty would make determined attempts to revert to her overdependence, whimpering reproachfully at being deserted. Then she would use baby talk and refuse—demonstratively and with tears—to continue her game. Again, this is quite unlike the unforthcoming child, who, at worst, just freezes. One could see that she was employing a strategy in an attempt to be babied by her mother. But when she found her strategy did not work she "snapped back into her usual happy self." Generally, she rose to the challenges of learning, was eager to please, and made good progress in the reading games; on one occasion she even continued beyond the finishing time. The result—except for her occasional attempted reversions to dependence—was an outgoing child.

How do the two criteria for congenitality apply to Betty's condition? Her birth was normal, but she cried all the next day and had a high temperature. On coming home, she cried a great deal and wanted to be walked about all the time, and the mother and grandmother spent hours each night doing this. This excessive need for mothering could have been an early manifestation of what later became overdependence.

Betty's developmental milestones were normal, but at three and a half years she developed a speech defect, such that even her parents could understand little of what she said. At sixteen months she had a severe bowel infection, followed by a minor convulsion in which she went stiff. The same kind of convulsion was repeated at three years, when she had tonsilitis. She suffered from an ear problem which was corrected by surgery when she was five. Her health history shows, in summary, the proneness to diverse impairments which is characteristic of the congenitally affected child. It also suggests that she suffered periods of pain and discomfort, which no doubt heightened her excessive dependence on her mother.

Four-year-old *Jean* was an extreme case of overdependence. In a Nursery for the retarded, she would do nothing but lie on the floor sucking her thumb and waiting for her favorite volunteer helper to pick her up and nurse her like a baby. Her mother reported similar behavior at home; she also had temper tantrums followed by sulking when she could not get her own way. What was even more surprising was that at home she played with her younger brother and even took the lead. The mother nevertheless accepted that Jean was retarded, and she reinforced her overdependence in much the same way as did the Nursery helpers.

The first step in Jean's treatment was to put an end to this reinforcement of her dependence strategy. Left to lie on the floor, within a few days she made her way over to the toy corner and was soon interacting with other children. Her progress to normality (documented step by step elsewhere[14],[15]) began when she was brought into a group of three other children in the Retarded Nursery who were beginning the Flying Start program.[8] Given the half pictures of the Two-Piece Puzzles, she showed no sign of comprehending what was expected of her, and she resisted all cajoling to participate. If it had been an IQ test, her behavior would indeed have earned her a rating of retardate. The two halves of one of the puzzles were then placed almost joined in front of her. Momentarily forgetting her strategy of non-participation, she pushed them together. She was lavishly praised, with the result that she did the same the next time and the next. Soon she was accepting the two halves given to her one after the other and joining them correctly. The next week she was doing the Four-Piece Puzzles. She began playing happily with the other children and even experimented in the use of an active, initiative taking lifestyle. A week later she was posting the alphabet cards in the Mailbox game. She exploited her new lifestyle to the point of being described as disruptive. She even laughed heartily, became competitive in the group activities, and meddlesome—just the opposite, in short, of the unforthcoming child and of her earlier extreme passivity.

The next week—as is typical in the rehabilitation of the dependent child—she had a partial relapse: the volunteer who had nursed her so lovingly returned after being away for several weeks, and the opportunity to be babied once more was too good to miss. Nevertheless, when the volunteer had been briefed to refrain, Jean resumed her outgoing style. She sang a verse of a song by herself in front of the other children and the staff of the Nursery, and she became elated at being able to say her numbers from one to ten.

At this time—some two months after the beginning of the treatment—she obtained an above average score on the Effectiveness-Motivation Scale.[16] By the next week she was giving ample evidence of her high effectiveness-motivation. At the swimming pool, not only did she undress and dress herself, but she tried to help dress an adult volunteer. She jumped into the pool willingly and bobbed her head under water, which would have been quite unthinkable for an unforthcoming child.

It was realized that Jean should be taken out of the Retarded Nursery and placed with the five year olds in our Centre. As soon as she arrived, she decided to try out her earlier dependence strategy; she whined for her mother and refused to participate in activities which she had previously enjoyed. Another child shamed her out of it by asking her, "Do you want to come and play or stand there crying?" The alternation of coping styles continued, but the dependent, pouting phases became less frequent. Intellectually, she made great strides, showing no lack of confidence. When she completed the Flying Start she began the reading program and surprised us by her rapid mastery of phonics.

Soon after entering the first year Infants class Jean reverted to her stubborn, dependent mood. She and her mother went into a residential treatment center for a few weeks, where the mother was trained not to reinforce her dependence. Five years later Jean was rated as an average pupil in an ordinary school.

It may be asked whether Jean's overdependence was anything more than the result of the mother's reinforcement. Whereas this undoubtedly allowed Jean to carry her strategy to such an extreme, it could not have been the sole cause. The mother had four other children, none of whom showed the trait. Many mothers continue to baby their children, but children of normal effectiveness motivation take pride in breaking away from the state of dependence, insisting on feeding and dressing themselves, wanting to do things unaided, and generally having control of their own actions. Paradoxically, Jean had high effectiveness-motivation, but her need for mothering was even greater, and it had become the dominant motivation of her life.

In effect, Jean's early history was typical of the multiple-impaired child. After a breech birth, she was incubated for 48 hours owing to mucous congestion. For some days she was jaundiced and lay passive without moving her limbs. At two and a half years she suffered a single, major epileptic seizure. Her developmental milestones were extremely retarded. She did not crawl until twelve months, nor walk across the room unaided before twenty seven months. She began to put two or three words together at twenty four months, but at four years she had such jumbled speech that it was sometimes difficult to understand her.

The most telltale impairment in understanding Jean's abnormal dependency needs was that she did not smile or show any other evidence of appreciating affection until the age of eighteen months—normally an infant shows the first signs of smiling by three weeks or earlier, and by six weeks is responding to maternal stimulation with full smiles. With the onset of her affectional responses Jean became very clinging; she could not bear to have her mother or other members of the family out of her sight. At about two years she lost her unnatural placidity and developed her pattern of tantrums and sulking. It is tempting to conclude that she was belatedly making her way through the infantile phase of extreme dependency while, at the same time, learning strategies for punishing her mother whenever she felt she was not getting sufficient attention. The mother, with her overindulgent and anxious temperament, reinforced these dependency strategies by continuing to baby the child.

Jean's pose of retardation was so convincing that she would undoubtedly have remained a "retardate" but for exposure to the treatment program. With the general readiness to jump to a diagnosis of retardation, one has to ask how many other children are thus labeled when their handicap is one of a temperamental dependency or other behavior disturbance.

SCHOOL REFUSAL

The stubbornness noted in the two overdependent children already described sometimes takes the form of a refusal to go to school. This is commonly called "school phobia," but the term misleadingly suggests some irrational and unconscious compulsion. It is better to think of school phobia as a strategy by which the child achieves some goal, remaining under the mother's wing rather than being exposed to teachers who may

not be so sympathetic and to other children who demand robust partici-
pation in play activities. The resistance of the child to cajoling and persua-
sion strengthens the idea that school refusal is the manifestation of some
deep psychiatric malady. The ability of the school refuser to hold out so
long is rather evidence of the child's confidence in the effectiveness of the
strategy, which is, of course, reinforced by the concern which adults mani-
fest over it. This view is supported by the general experience that if a
strange adult comes to the home one morning and says to the child,
"Come along, we are going to school this morning" and simply takes the
child off in a car, the strategy is abandoned and the child goes to school
without ill effects from then on. It may be necessary to place an older
school refuser in a residential center for a week or two; from there the
child can go to school with the other children.

The fact that the school refuser has so much confidence in the success of the strategy indicates that it and similar strategies—resorting to
tantrums and feigned physical incapacities—have been successful when
used on the mother. It will, therefore, probably be necessary to brief her
in detail about how to deal with the tantrums, the feeding difficulties, and
the leg and stomach aches that she has previously given in to.

While school refusal is predominantly a manifestation of overdependence, it would be dangerous to assume that this is always the case.
We have learned not to tie any one symptom to a particular type of behavior disturbance. Truancy is the classic example of behavior which
appears frequently in connection with hostility, avoidance-compulsion,
and impulsivity, so that all we can say of it is that it is an indication of
some sort of overreacting maladjustment. When a mother asks, "What does
it mean when a child does so-and-so?" the correct answer is, "Tell me
about some of the other things your child does."

EATING DIFFICULTIES

When I was studying the behavior of children in small institutions, I used
to ask about fussiness and other difficulties in eating. I got the forthright
answer, "We never have any." I assured myself that this was not because of
strict discipline but because of the fact that when there are twenty children
of about the same age, making difficulties over eating is not a good strategy
for exercising power over adults. On the other hand, mothers who find it

difficult to hide their concern about whether the child is getting enough to eat tend to be easy victims of this strategy. The simple counterstrategy is to let the child refuse to eat—at the same time, making sure that no food of inferior nutritive value is substituted—and, above all, to ban all eating between meals.

This advice must be tempered by the realization that eating is subject to instinctive likes and dislikes which go far back into our evolution. In some children, certain foods—tapioca, ground rice, tripe, milk with the skin on it—touch off instinctive aversions against swallowing foreign bodies and may cause them to throw up.

Many parents insist that their children eat green vegetables because they are good for them. The fact that it is rare to find a child who eats them willingly indicates that this is also an instinctive dislike—albeit not such an intense one—which may extend through adolescence. The evolutionary value of it was, I believe, that when our ancestors were still hominids, the older and dominant members of the group had priority for any food available and the young got only what was left over (as is the case now with the large beasts of prey). The young had, therefore, to bolt down those foods containing abundant carbohydrates and proteins—such as are necessary for a highly active life—before an adult drove them off. It would have been a waste of valuable time to eat green plant food. This also explains why adolescents bolt their food and prefer that which is easily gulped down, such as white bread, doughnuts, hot dogs, and hamburgers.

chapter eight

Handicaps
of temperament
Inconsequence ("hyperactivity")
and affectional unconcern

FAILURE TO THINK AHEAD

At its most primitive level, behavior is merely a matter of responding to a present stimulus: a hen sees a grain of corn and pecks it up; a rabbit runs away from a fox. But if one of us were to respond to every present stimulus as if nothing else mattered, we should soon be in deep trouble. In the brain of the normal person there is some mechanism for reviewing the wider consequences of each proposed action before it is carried out. If these consequences are seen to have undesired results, we refrain from the act, however sorely tempted we may be. We all know the feeling of, "What I should like to do, or say, to that person"—yet we manage to hold ourselves back from doing or saying what would have unwelcome consequences. This ability to inhibit undesirable actions is an important element in adjustment.

All the reactive types of maladjustment involve a failure to inhibit self-injurious behavior. It has been seen that in the effort to block distressing memories children may resort to irrational behavior that gets them into trouble. Hostile children commit provocative acts that antagonize people against them. Apart from those who react against an emotionally intolerable situation, there are children who are temperamentally inclined to act without considering the consequences. They fall into two broad types.

THE HIGH-EFFECTIVENESS INCONSEQUENT

The first type of temperamental inconsequent has an overpowering need to react dramatically with the world and to produce spectacular effects in order to make his or her presence felt; these children have a stronger effectiveness motivation than they can control. They try to achieve every result too fast, and they insist on doing everything their own way. Consequently, they get into learning difficulties by not taking the time to examine a problem carefully and by not accepting guidance from adults. Because of their high activity level and lack of interest in routine tasks at school, they are often diagnosed as hyperactive or perceptually handicapped. In effect, they usually show exceptionally good perceptual ability when they choose to use it, and they can pay close attention to what interests them. They are, however, bored with routine tasks.

Some children of this type develop special talents, notably a verbal or artistic ability beyond their years. Indeed, with their insistence on working out solutions in their own way, these children—if they can acquire the necessary discipline—become the creative people of the future. Their problem is that they tend to tire their parents, make themselves unpopular with other children by their forwardness and interfering, and get on the wrong side of their teachers. It is significant that—in the study by Hutt and Bhavnani previously referred to—the subsequent classroom behavior of two of the five girls who had been "Inventive Explorers" as preschoolers was rated by their primary teachers as undesirable; and the ten "Inventive Explorer" boys were found by their teachers to be "disruptive influences in the classroom." Dr. Marie O'Neill[1] describes a five-year-old boy who, in between the fitting of the pieces of a puzzle, would run round the classroom on the tops of the desks, each time stopping for a second or two to fit the next piece, which he did with unfailing accuracy.

In the preschool center for the retarded, four-year-old *Andrew's* favorite activity was riding his tricycle in and out among the other children; he did this skillfully and at great speed. If spoken to, he replied with a shout and continued babbling nonsense to himself. It was evident from his first efforts to do the Two-Piece Puzzles[2] that he was unpracticed in understanding pictures, and he found this activity too slow and unrewarding. He seemed a typical hyperactive child with poor perceptual skills. Nevertheless, he quickly got the idea of posting the alphabet cards in the mailboxes[2] and, once reminded not to try to work too fast, he did so correctly. Then he began to help a slower child, showing her in which boxes to post the cards and scolding her loudly when she disobeyed him. He proceeded to teach other children, paying close attention to their efforts and correcting them when necessary. In a stores game he showed excellent play-fantasy (one of the criteria of high effectiveness motivation). A little later, in the reading program, he quickly mastered the phonic principle. When the teacher said, "L for leaf," he replied "Like Linda." (He can be seen playing with the Touch Cards of the Programmed Reading Kit successfully in the film "Learning to Learn"[3]).

By his limited vocabulary, babyish speech, and excessive activity, Andrew had given the Health Visitor who came to his home the impression that he was retarded. If given an IQ test, he probably would not have agreed to cooperate or would not have troubled to listen to or look at the tasks. His social background was such that he heard little speech and saw no pictures. Physical activity was the only outlet for his strong effectiveness-motivation.

THE NEURALLY
IMPAIRED INCONSEQUENT

Inconsequent children of the second type do not possess this ability to concentrate upon what interests them. They are at the mercy of every passing stimulus. Since they neither reflect on the results of their actions nor recall what happened when they did the same thing last time, they learn little from their experiences. In psychological terms, they are hard to condition.

Hugh, at seven years, was an example of the nearly unconditionable sort of inconsequent. His teachers found him likeable, but he was a disturber of the peace for whom there seemed no answer. Punishment was no deterrent, and he quickly forgot without holding a grudge. He fell into a canal and was pulled out unconscious, but he showed no concern and soon after regaining consciousness wanted to go out and play again. He was always on the look out for mischief, starting rough play, misbehaving when the teacher was out of the room, and accepting dares to perform risky pranks. In his work he lacked concentration and made no effort to be neat.

CONGENITALITY OF SOME INCONSEQUENCE

The prevalence of multiple impairment among inconsequent children leads us to believe that in many of them the condition is congenital. Nearly four times as many inconsequent as not-inconsequent children suffer from additional physical, neurological, and health handicaps. Besides their liabiliity to speech defects, they are three times more likely to be motor impaired than non-inconsequents.[4] Other authorities have noted the greater prevalence of a number of health and developmental disorders in hyperactive children, notably colic, abnormal activity level in the first year—which may be either undue passivity or restlessness—delays in "milestones," squint, speech defects, and seizures.[5]

It would, however, be a mistake to assume that all inconsequent children suffer from brain dysfunction. Many of them are nimble and athletic. In the Canadian survey which found so much motor impairment among inconsequent children, 31 percent of them nevertheless had above average motor ability. It is evident that inconsequence is in the nature of a conglomerate of conditions of different origins, that share the common feature of reckless and often disruptive initiative. It is reasonable to suppose that the well coordinated, healthy inconsequents belong to the first type, whose handicap—if it can be called that—is a degree of effectiveness motivation beyond their control. On the other hand, the poorly coordinated, unhealthy and motor impaired inconsequents are those of the second type; they suffer from a congenital multiple impairment which includes brain dysfunction.

It would, however, be risky to allocate inconsequents to one type or another entirely by the presence or absence of collateral impairments. There will always be some children who have but a single handicap, namely the brain dysfunction responsible for their disorganized behavior. Nevertheless, these collateral impairments, when present, make it more likely that the behavior disturbance derives from dysfunction of the mechanisms for monitoring the consequences of actions.

EXPLORING CONDITIONABILITY

The most reliable means of differentiating between the neurally intact, get-there-too-quick inconsequent and the inconsequent suffering from brain dysfunction is to work with children in a program designed to condition them to resist distracting stimuli and to delay their responses so that they have time to attend and reflect. Such a program is described in the section on treatment. Provided their interest can be maintained, children whose brains are functioning normally learn to concentrate within a very short time. Dr. Marie O'Neill found with her sample of four- and five-year-old children referred for learning problems that a group reached a stage where they showed no faults of learning style—in the form of distractibility or attentional deficit—after only three half-hours in the remedial program.[1] In contrast, the neurally impaired inconsequent cannot focus his or her attention or work steadily toward the solution of a problem at any time. It is not that no progress can be made with these children; but progress has to be slow, and, of course, discouraging to those who do not appreciate their handicap.

OBJECTIONS TO
THE TERM "HYPERACTIVITY"

The popular term for the kinds of behavior disturbance described in this chapter is "hyperactivity." This is, however, a misnomer. It has been pointed out that so called hyperactive children do not have a greater energy output than normally active children. They just give the impression of being excessively active by their frequent switches of activity and by the attention their behavior attracts. The activity of the good child, engaged in an acceptable, purposeful activity, is apt to pass unnoticed. Moreover, the most physically active of all are the high-effectiveness, get-there-too-quick inconsequents with normal brain function. The neurally impaired child is often subject to periods of lassitude, that is to say, *hypo*activity.

A second objection to thinking of these types of behavior disturbance as hyperactivity is that the activity level of children is, in part, determined by their upbringing and cultural-ethnic background. Chinese children show less exuberant activity than Black children. Children of the present generation are, as a whole, less inhibited than those of the Victorian and Edwardian eras. In a relatively permissive culture—in which the old saying, "Children should be seen and not heard," would be considered repressive—much more boisterous play has to be expected. The sight of sons sparring and wrestling with fathers or rough and tumble play between boys and girls would have been unthinkable two generations ago and still is in Chinese families. It is understandable that children raised in a culture that emphasizes spontaneous expression rather than inhibition may be unaccustomed to sitting still and listening, and if the discipline is lax will seize opportunities for more active sorts of fun. To judge by the speed with which some children diagnosed as hyperactive reduce their activity level and apply themselves to their tasks in a behavior modification program—and revert to their hyperactivity as soon as it is terminated—there is reason to believe that many children diagnosed as hyperactive are suffering only from a lack of discipline.

Hyperactivity can, in fact, become a cultural norm. People think less about the consequences of their acts when they are in a crowd. If the irresponsible, boisterous behavior of some children goes unchecked—and they are well-adjusted, popular children—others will follow them, and a large group may turn inconsequent.

A final objection to the continued use of the word "hyperactivity" is that—in the United States at least—it has become tied to drug therapy. In speaking to a group of American special education teachers a few years ago, I was astonished to learn from them that all the children in their classes were on drugs designed to control hyperactivity.

INATTENTIVENESS

Some authorities[6] see a constitutional lack of attention as the basic characteristic of children termed hyperactive. However, this is probably an aspect of a more general failure to filter out distracting stimuli. In order to be able to concentrate on a task, it is necessary *not* to attend to anything else. If the inhibitory mechanisms are defective, distracting stimuli cannot be blocked from consciousness. Thus, children who suffer from this type of brain dysfunction cannot exercise a selective attention. Inhibitional failure indeed affects normal people under conditions of fatigue. Some find that when tired they cannot tolerate noise, or their clothing feels uncomfortable. Others become verbally hyperactive or make hasty, ill considered decisions.

Another reason why hyperactivity cannot be simply defined as a failure to focus attention on a task is that neurally intact children can also be habitually inattentive. This applies to high-effectiveness inconsequents because they are bored with what is going on in the classroom and are occupied with their own thoughts or physical initiatives. Some children have never learned to attend to the subject matter of school learning; the emotionally deprived tend to be inattentive because their lessons offer them no solution to their anxieties. We have to learn to distinguish between, on the one hand, a constitutional inability to pay attention arising from brain dysfunction and, on the other, a lack of motivation to pay attention or lack of training in attention. This differential diagnosis can be made only when children are in a situation in which they want to pay attention in order to achieve some satisfaction, or, at least, in which normal children find enough interest and enjoyment that they pay attention spontaneously. Bruner[7] has remarked how, in their play, quite young children will concentrate and persevere for a surprisingly long time. How children play depends, in part, on their play habits and the kinds of toys they have. Consequently, the final diagnosis cannot be reached until the child has had opportunities to play with materials that invite attention and perceptual discrimination. Only when we see that the child cannot give attention to anything are we on sure ground in diagnosing brain dysfunction.

THE TREATMENT OF
THE INCONSEQUENT
(HYPERACTIVE) CHILD

One of the themes of this book is that, for regular success in treatment, we need to understand the nature of the condition. When it comes to the treatment of these impulsive children—whether we call them inconsequent or hyperactive—the first necessity is to assess the probability of brain dysfunction. In a few cases, there will be clear neurological indications. In many, however, the dysfunction affects only the higher brain centers which exercise a constant check on the consequences of each proposed act. In such cases there will be no other neurological signs, and the dysfunction can be diagnosed only by testing the child's ability to control behavior.

An ability to improve is more important than the state in which we find the child. Yet we cannot expect the child to improve spontaneously. The style of behavior is the child's way of compensating for the handicap. Distractibility is resorted to as a means of avoiding confrontation with failure. Consequently, the child has to be enticed out of this developmental blind alley by offering activities in which there is a good prospect of success and where failure is not critical. The child must not feel cornered in yet another academic exercise.

In the Guelph Center, we built the training into games.[8] Each game was designed in a way that if the children gave the necessary attention and delayed their response until they had thought out the answer, they would be rewarded by success, while thoughtless guessing was "punished" by failure. The program was graded so that at the beginning only a minimal amount of attention was required. In the later stages, the games demanded close attention and the thinking out of answers.

In such game activities it will be found that the high effectiveness type of inconsequent learns the correct strategies quickly. They abandon their earlier style of guessing, and they adopt an attentive, reflective style of learning which assures them regular success. The early part of the film "Learning to Learn" shows two undoubtedly hyperactive children of this type playing the Mailbox game. One of them throws a box under the table for the other to retrieve. He hits the other over the head. Then he discovers by accident that he can make the alphabet cards stick on his forearm, so he practices lifting them off the table in this way, forgetting all about the game he is meant to be playing. Apart from the unorthodox and often disruptive ways in which he achieved effectivness, his learning was hindered by his continual limb movements. These were not due to nervous disease because he could control them when he wanted to. They seemed rather an expression of the impatience of the high-effectiveness child, as if his urges to activity were set on too fine a spring. Later in the film—when he has realized that the game had possibilities for success that were within his grasp—he is seen concentrating and posting the alphabet cards in the right boxes.

This boy's restlessness was subsequently cured with the help of his mother, who worked as a volunteer in the Center. Continually telling him not to fidget was not specific enough, so we began with his feet. His mother told him that he would do well at the game if he kept his feet still. He took this literally, and in the effort to control the fidgetting with his feet, he controlled all his fidgets. This enabled him to succeed in the games, and he extended his new learning style to his learning in general. From then on, he began to do very well in school.

The purpose of the learning-to-learn games that these boys were playing is to teach them the skills required in school: to pay close attention, to think out solutions, and to have confidence in their abilities. In order to do well at them it is necessary to keep the body and limbs reasonably still, although the manipulation of the cards involved moving the arms and, to some extent, the body. Thus, in playing them, the children learn that concentration on a task and reflecting about their choices involves control of random movement. They acquire these learning skills not by being told to use their eyes or to stop and think or to keep still, but by constantly finding themselves in situations in which a good learning strategy brings success and a poor one brings failure. It is a matter of conditioning them by letting them see the outcome of their various behaviors.

One cannot, nevertheless, assume that the good learning and problem solving habits developed in these games will be automatically transferred to school tasks. Much depends on the nature of the tasks they are given in school. If they consist of the repetitive and boring completion of work books and similar tasks—without immediate knowledge of the result of their efforts—it is understandable that many will revert to tactics of distraction and disruptiveness.

The logical solution to this problem of transfer is to build the teaching of the basic skills of reading, writing, and arithmetic into programs of learning games; in this way, the children continue to be reinforced by being able to see immediately whether they are right or wrong in each and every response. In the Guelph Center, such programs carried some of the children through to fluent reading and mastery of the basic arithmetical processes. No sudden transfer to different kinds of activity took place. Once, however, the children find they can read, they feel encouraged to practice their skill spontaneously outside the program.

Inconsequent children require training in forethought in their daily lives as well as in school tasks. They are the kind of children who run out from behind parked cars or are dared to throw stones at windows. They tend to be excluded from the group games which their peers organize because they fool around and cannot wait their turn. Their skills at these games also tend to be poor; in some of them it is because of their motor impairment, in others because their impatience prevents them from following a proper sequence of bodily movements. The same can apply to the sequencing of their speech. The typical inconsequent speaks in an impatient, jumbled manner; as their parents say, they try to get all the words out at once, and they have to be told to slow down so that people can understand them.

For the training that inconsequent children need in physical activity, there is no need to put them through formal exercises. In any case, unless they are motivated to do their best, they will fail to note what brings success and no learning will take place. Many children's games provide natural opportunities for learning bodily control, the judging of distance, keeping an objective in mind, and the self-discipline of team membership. For bodily control there are hopscotch, skipping, walking on a plank or bar, and Mary Wignall's action rhymes.[9] Hide-and-seek requires the ability to remain motionless; it and the treasure hunt give an advantage to those who can focus their attention and stop to think which are the most probable hiding places. Ball games combine many sorts of training, from the estimation of distance to the self-restraint involved in awaiting one's turn and faithfully performing the less glamorous roles. Swimming is, of course, an excellent trainer in movement control. Domestic card games place a premium on attention and the thinking out of strategies. There is, in short, no lack of physical and other recreational activities which can help the inconsequent. The chief thing is to ensure that the child's clumsiness—or the unpopularity arising from disruptive behavior—do not lead to avoidance of recreational activities.

For some of the speech defects of inconsequent children, professional therapy is needed. For those whose poor speech is merely a matter of trying to say too much too quickly, the natural forms of training afforded by acting and games involving asking and answering questions should be sufficient.

BEHAVIOR MODIFICATION

Behavior modification, originating with B. F. Skinner, has had a great popularity in recent years; it has been seen by some as the long awaited answer to behavior problems. Skinner extended Pavlov's theory of conditioning to the field of learning, while retaining Watson's denial of any role for consciousness and insight. For him, learning occurred when two events—such as an act and its outcome—occurred in close succession, so that the animal could make the connection and repeat the behavior in order to be further rewarded. Animal trainers have, of course, used this method of teaching from time immemorial, and knowledge of the outcome is part of the spontaneous learning that occurs in everyday life. In this respect, it might be described as natural learning, but it is unnatural if the incentive is provided by an external agent, who, by applying or withholding the reward, controls the behavior.

Behavior modifiers give children either material reinforcement—in the form either of goodies or of tokens which they can exchange for treats—or privileges. They do not aim to build any reward into the activity itself, which may remain boring or distasteful. Indeed, behavior modifiers demonstrate the effectiveness of their methods by showing that the original, undesirable behavior is resumed as soon as the supply of goodies is discontinued.

The limitations of behavior modification become apparent when we consider the emotional deprivations which lie behind the reactive forms of behavior disturbance. A child who feels rejected by his parents, or who is desperately anxious about the possibility that his mother will desert the home, will be indifferent to small material rewards in the form of goodies or tokens. It is not fortuitous that behavior modifiers refrain from looking into the reasons for undesirable behavior. Their assumption is that all these reasons are a matter of faulty previous conditioning—that some children have not learned that if they do things other people dislike they will be punished.

For this reason, behavior modification has been most successful in controlling disruptive behavior in the classroom, which—in a permissive society—may often be due to lack of discipline. What distinguishes maladjusted children from their normal, even if unruly, classmates is that they do not respond to any sort of incentive to good behavior.

Behavior modification is equally ineffective in the treatment of the underreacting forms of maladjustment. Material incentives will not give confidence to the temperamentally unforthcoming child, nor will they stimulate the depressed child, and they will not cure the withdrawal which arises from severe and prolonged deprivation or affectional unconcern.

Nevertheless, behavior modification—or perhaps we should say the application of the general principle that desirable behavior is rewarded—is appropriate for the treatment of some kinds of behavior problems. At the Guelph Center for Educational Disabilities, when a mother complained that she could not control her hyperactive boy (of the enterprising, high-effectiveness type) we recommended that she pay him his weekly allowance by daily installments (when he is already in bed for the night)—the timing being important because getting the child to bed is one of the parent's chief problems. The mother was advised to explain to him that he will receive the full daily amount only if he has behaved himself, and she was told to make it clear which kinds of behavior she considers desirable or undesirable. For each lapse, a small part of the daily allowance is deducted. Except for a most heinous offense, it should not be reduced to nothing—for then the child will reason that he may as well be hanged for a sheep as for a goat. If, after deduction, the child does something exceptionally nice, it may be restored. After the mother of one particularly active and impulsive boy had applied this form of behavior modification for some three weeks, she came back to the Center in a state of great concern: her son had become so good that she was sure there must be something wrong with him!

It will be recalled also that Jean, the overdependent child, was successfully treated by a kind of behavior modification program. This consisted in ceasing to reinforce her strategy of helplessness, and rewarding her with praise once she began to participate in the learning games.

In conclusion, the kinds of maladjustment for which behavior modification is an appropriate form of treatment are those in which the maladjusted behavior is more a strategy than a compulsion. The strategies both of the inconsequent (or hyperactive) child of the high effectiveness type—who tries to "push the world around"—and of the overdependent child—who controls adults by helplessness—afford them much immediate gratification but are detrimental to their long term interests. Although these behavior patterns have their origin in handicaps of temperament, they are nevertheless sufficiently within the children's control to enable them to adapt to a situation which offers gratifications of a different type. This form of real life behavior modification is thus an aspect of situational treatment.

It follows from this discussion that to indiscriminately apply behavior modification to all kinds of maladjustment is to invite failure in the great majority of cases. Success—beyond the level of good luck—entails the ability to recognize the various types of maladjustment and to understand their causes.

The learning games described in this and in the previous chapter are a form of conditioning, and they follow the behavior modification principle of immediate knowledge of the result of each act. They differ, however, in the nature of the reward. All that the goodies or tokens of a traditional behavior modification teach children is that if they act in the desired way in a particular situation they will get the reward. Because the activity itself offers them nothing, they will, quite logically, revert to their previous behavior pattern once the source of reinforcement dries up. If, on the other hand, the activity carries its own rewards—making the children feel more competent—they will need no externally offered incentive. They then progressively discover that certain strategies—deciding to participate, concentrating, thinking ahead, testing alternative solutions—are followed by success. The same strategies apply in games of different sorts as well as in everyday life, so that every extension of them to a new activity is also rewarded. In this way, children can be conditioned to new and more effective styles of coping, and they can be weaned away from those which are ineffective, pathological, or illicit.

CONTROLLING "HYPERACTIVITY"
BY DRUGS

In the United States there has been what can only be described as the reckless use of drugs to control the disorganized behavior diagnosed by hyperactivity. The drugs given to calm the children down and make them more attentive are, paradoxically, stimulants. Their action is presumably to activate the behavior controlling mechanisms which are in a state of dysfunction. Their attractiveness is that they often bring about a reduction in disruptive and distractible behavior, much to the relief of parents and teachers.

There are weighty objections to drug therapy as the standard mode of treatment. The first is that diagnosis is so haphazard that many more children are labeled (and drugged) as hyperactive than suffer from brain dysfunction. What many of them need is nothing more than training in the control of their behavior and in good study habits.

A second objection to the general use of drugs is that, so long as children are under their influence, they have no opportunity of learning to control their behavior by natural means. The sort of conditioning program described previously—in which acts of attention are reinforced and children see the ineffectiveness of random guessing—would be rendered useless because learning in the drugged state is not transferred to the natural state. When the drug is discontinued, the children are thrown by distractions and do not know how to deal with their hasty impulses. Advocates of drug use admit this, but they reply that the drugging must therefore be continued indefinitely. They justify their refusal to use any form of training in the control of behavior by declaring that it does not work. It is true that, at present, there is little formal evidence of success in working directly on the child's behavior; but this is because few attempts have been made to do so owing to the pessimism generated by the drug advocates.

Reinforcement methods, such as those described previously, will at least serve to prevent neurally intact overactive children from being indefinitely drugged. In our Center—to which many young children diagnosed as hyperactive were referred—control of behavior and good work habits were achieved with all but a very few who were severely affected, and even with these, progress was discernible. Stimulant drugs were never used. In conclusion, there seems a reasonable prospect—once behavioral means of treatment become better known—of dispensing with drug treatment (except to halt a deterioration in parent-child relationships when the child has so got on his parents' nerves that there is a risk that they will no longer be able to control *their* behavior).

PHYSICAL REASONS
FOR INCONSEQUENCE

The third objection to the use of drugs in controlling hyperactivity is that—as the pediatrician Walker[10] has pointed out—they merely mask the symptoms without curing the disease. The logic of his approach is that if there are signs of brain dysfunction, such as grossly uncontrolled behavior, it makes sense to find out what is causing it. Since oxygen is the most critical element in normal brain functioning, he looked for disorders that could interfere with the supply of oxygen to the brain. Among these are heart disease and other malfunction of the circulatory system: he quotes the case of a hyperactive girl whose behavior became normal after an operation on an obstruction impeding the flow of blood between the heart and lung. In other cases, the causes of the brain dysfunction were a deficiency of glucose in the blood, calcium deficiency (cured by the child's drinking more milk), glandular dysfunction, lead or carbon monoxide poisoning, and brain injury. He also found purely incidental causes such as uncomfortable underwear and hunger. It is interesting that Walker also mentions "strong curiosity," which was his way of describing high effectiveness motivation.

Many inconsequent, distractible children complain of stomach, head, or leg aches; these are often regarded as part of their attention seeking or as ways of evading school tasks, as well they may sometimes be. But other possibilities have to be considered. The pains and the behavior disturbance may both be symptoms of a food or other allergy. If other signs of inhibitional dysfunction are observed, such as being too easily startled (the inability to inhibit "jumpy" reactions to unexpected noises or to the sudden appearance of another person) there may be a similar inability to ignore minor pains and discomforts. Alternatively—as I believe to have been the case in one extremely restless three-year-old boy—the child may be suffering chronic pain, which is kept from consciousness by constant hyperactivity in the same way as an older child may try to avoid the memory of a distressing family situation.

If it is suspected that the pain may be real, yet no physical cause for it can be discovered, the possibility that the pain and the hyperactivity are caused by an allergy should be explored.

The possible effects of allergic reactions to food coloring have, in recent years, been put forward energetically by Dr. Feingold,[11] and he has won a number of enthusiastic followers among parents who claim that the elimination of coloring matter from their children's food has resulted in the cessation of the disorganized behavior. The earlier independent controlled studies failed to establish any such general connection, but more recent research has shown that the large quantities of coloring matter in the diet of some children can cause nervous symptoms.

The recently reported work of Crook[12] makes it highly probable that coloring matter is only one of several food allergens that can produce inconsequence, and this could account for the lack of clear statistical confirmation of the effects of coloring matter studied in isolation. Among the children whom he had treated as patients, Crook ascertained from the replies of 136 parents to his questionnaire that the behavior disturbance of 70 percent was definitely related to specific foods in their diet, and the condition improved when the foods in question were eliminated. Another 5 percent showed improvement on the elimination diet, but it could not be attributed to a specific food. Nine percent showed the "hyperactivity" as probably related to diet, and in only 4½ percent was there no apparent relationship. The following were the chief foods causing "hyperactivity": sugar in 77 children; colors, additives, and flavors in 48; milk in 38; corn (maize) in 30; chocolate in 28; egg in 20; wheat in 15; potato in 13; soy bean in 12; citrus in 11; and pork in 10. Crook's was a highly selected sampling because, as an allergist, all his cases had allergies of some kind; some of the 53 parents who did not reply may have done so because the results were negative. Nevertheless, he seems to have established a case for exploring the possibility of food allergies—of many different kinds and not only from coloring matter—in all inconsequent children. The procedure he advocates is to eliminate a number of suspect foods from the child's diet for seven to ten days. To identify the offending food, the eliminated items are reinstated one at a time. Each would be removed and reinstated at least twice more in order to make sure that the effect was not fortuitous. He states that improvement will be shown for most of the affected children within five days, but in some 20 percent it will take 8 to 14 days.

It becomes abundantly clear that, with all these possibilities, the diagnosis of the causes, and hence the treatment, of inconsequence can be lengthy and expensive. Since there is no point in subjecting healthy and neurologically intact children—who need nothing more than training in the control of their behavior and in positive learning skills—to the medical procedures, the first stage in the exploration of causes should be a course of behavioral remediation. Only if the inability of the child to make progress points to the likelihood of brain dysfunction, would it be necessary to embark upon the specialized medical explorations advocated by Walker and Crook.

AFFECTIONAL UNCONCERN

Alec knew the difference between right and wrong, but it did not concern him. Being on people's "bad lists" caused him no anxiety because he lacked the desire for personal attachments which is the foundation of good conduct. This freedom from anxiety meant that—unlike the hostile child or the compulsive avoider—he could carry out his crimes with all his wits about him. He knew that adults took strong exception to stealing, but this only made him more calculating. He stole a money box from a nursery school, and he maintained his denial with cool lies until identified by several women. He kept his coolness even when all the evidence was against him. Although a boy scout himself, he led a gang in breaking into a boy scout hut. In the course of the subsequent investigation his attitude was, "I can't understand why you're questioning me." He stole whiskey from a shopkeeper for whom he worked, and he exchanged it for cake with some boys who worked in a bakery. He knew he would not be prosecuted because, being only 13 years of age, he was illegally employed on licensed premises. He also took money from the till, no doubt thinking it would be put down to someone's error. He stole repeatedly both in and out of school but managed to escape being charged because he was "such a nice little boy."

In school, Alec was not disruptive like an inconsequent or morose and antagonistic like a hostile child. On the contrary, he was "a charming rogue," glib and plausible, and he knew how to manipulate personal relationships. He could even behave better, as a matter of policy, when corrected. But the teachers knew that before long another of his misdemeanors would come to light—some new act of stealing or spitefulness to weaker children.

Alec's calculating amorality stood in sharp contrast to the antisocial behavior of the boys described in Chapter 3 who had reacted to extreme deprivation by a general affectional withdrawal. Their overpowering enmity against the world had prevented them from getting along with people even when it was in their interest to do so. Affectionally unconcerned children like Alec can get along with people, but they do so only to take advantage of them. On superficial acquaintance, they give the appearance of normality, but their lack of empathy for the feelings of others causes them to make miscalculations by which they expose themselves. Like the classical gangster, Alec would brag and play the hero—his lack of anxiety about his good standing with his peers allowed him this easy form of personal effectiveness.

The handicap of temperament from which Alec suffered was one of affectional unconcern. There was nothing to appeal to in him; approval was no reward and disapproval no punishment. If it was a congenital defect it must have consisted in dysfunction of those mechanisms which are the seat of the almost universal need in children for social attachments.

It will be recalled that the probability of the congenital origin of disturbed behavior can be gauged by two criteria: the first is the early appearance of abnormal behavior, especially of the type in question. How early "moral defect" such as Alec showed makes its appearances is difficult to say because young childen are normally egocentric; in the first stage of moral development right and wrong are equated with what one is allowed to do.[13] Alec's mother said that he had always been "different" from her other six children. Her only specific complaint about him was that he was consistently spiteful towards the younger ones; this started when he was six, on the birth of a brother.

The second criterion of congenitality is collateral impairments. Alec was a restless sleeper and a frequent bed wetter. His mother was very ill as a result of his birth—there might have been some complication which affected him.

Alec certainly suffered no deprivation of maternal love or care such as might conceivably have caused his incapacity for affection. His mother was a model of patience. She was not blind to his bad ways, but there was no hint that she rejected him. Moreover, her other children were affectionally normal and reasonably well behaved. Nor could his spitefulness be attributed to sibling jealousy. Many normal children will occasionally be jealous of, and even spiteful to, their younger siblings; but this is not projected into a general amorality in their social relationships. Alec's habitual spitefulness to children outside his own family is typical of the affectionally unconcerned child.

Affectional unconcern as an abnormality of personality must not be confused with the lack of concern that people commonly show towards outsiders or foreigners (those who are not members of the group they identify with, especially those they have never met and only know of as populations). Normal people can be unfeeling and cruel to strangers. The distinguishing characteristic of the affectionally unconcerned, psychopaths, or moral defectives—as they are variously called—is that they have no compunction about injuring those who are close to them and to whom they would normally be bound by bonds of comradeship or affection.

It has also to be recognized that otherwise decent human beings are prepared to do harm to other people—and even to their own kin—when driven by greed or ambition for power and position. It is also wrong to call these people psychopaths. A very strong motivation, whether good or bad, inhibits weaker motivations. The power or wealth seeker finds no difficulty in inhibiting his social feelings.

Likewise, the teenager who identifies with a group of his peers can behave in an antisocial manner—by vandalism or even personal injury—against strangers or an anonymous society without being a constitutional psychopath. Young people under the influence of an avoidance compulsion commit irresponsible acts without considering the harm they do. Their behavior is antisocial but not psychopathic in the strict sense of the word, which implies insensibility to right and wrong. In effect, the concept of psychopathy tends to be loosely used to include grossly antisocial behavior, whatever its motivation. It should be added that "antisocial" is also applied too widely to diverse sorts of maladjustment and is therefore, valueless as a diagnostic category. It does not help those responsible for the treatment of a maladjusted young person to be told that he is antisocial—they know that already—but it does help to know whether the antisocial behavior is indicative of hostility, avoidance compulsion, inconsequence, affectional unconcern, or normal group thoughtlessness.

THE TREATMENT OF THE
AFFECTIONALLY UNCONCERNED

Applied to affectionally unconcerned children, the word "treatment"—in the sense of an attempt to improve the condition—may arouse vain hopes. Because they have no need for human attachments—approval or disapproval mean nothing—there is little that can be offered them (except material rewards) for behaving in a socially acceptable manner. Material rewards will be accepted, and possibly worked for, as long as they are available, but they will have no general socializing effect. Ordinary punishments only make them more cunning, and they too have no general effect on their social attitudes. The most that can be done is to be ever watchful, so as to limit their opportunities for wrongdoing.

There is, however, a ray of hope for the parents of such a child (who is, fortunately, rare). At each stage of human life, growth is influenced by different sets of genetic instructions. This applies also to the genes influencing behavior. At puberty, it would appear that the young person gets what may amount to a brand new personality. It has been mentioned how unforthcoming, timid children can be transformed into aggressive adolescents. Likewise, a congenital indifference to affection at the pre-pubertal stage can be replaced in adolescence by a lively concern for fellow human beings. I have in mind a boy of about twelve years—a typical affectionless, amoral child—who, on his return from a correctional school at fourteen, showed the utmost concern for and tenderness toward his mother and other members of his family. He was only one of several in my experience in which this transformation took place. There are even grounds for believing that it may be the general rule. Of the entire series of 102 youths, aged fifteen to eighteen years, whom I studied intensively in a correctional school, [14] there were quite a few who had become hardened into a state of affectional withdrawal owing to the extremes of deprivation they had suffered. They stood out because of the grudge they felt against humanity, which so ruled them that they were unable, even in their own interests, to maintain any social relationship. But there was not one who could be called a "constitutional psychopath," in the sense that he was devoid of any human feeling and indifferent to social relationships.

The best advice, therefore, that can be given to the parents of a constitutionally affectionless child—after explaining to them the nature of the handicap—is to exercise the closest supervision possible and to use whatever deterrents, short of cruelty, they find have some effect; they must play a waiting game with the prospect that after puberty normal human feelings will emerge. It may, of course, be necessary for the child to be accommodated until this happens in a residential school equipped to handle maladjusted and deviant children.

chapter nine

Preventing
maladjustment

INDIVIDUAL VARIATIONS
IN VULNERABILITY

Occasionally, children remain well adjusted despite having been exposed to acutely depriving situations over most of their lives. Of the 108 children in Hilda Lewis's sample[1] of deprived children who had been permanently separated from their mothers before the age of five, eleven were found to be stable, even though they had not been wanted or loved by their parents and had, moreover, been brought up in institutions. The reasons for the normality of some of them was that other women had given them motherly care. However, a few were deprived even of this compensation. One was looked after from the age of two by a woman who was indifferent to her; another had been actually disliked by her fostermother; a third had been deserted by her mother at the age of a few months and had then lived with several relatives, none of whom wanted her. Lewis mentions, in particular, an adolescent girl who was taken into public care shortly after birth and had many changes of nursery institution. From the age of ten, she was placed in a foster home and, after further changes, was finally homeless and living in a Reception Center. There, her conduct was absolutely normal; she was an attractive, sociable girl who was adaptable and interested in people It is thus evident that even extreme deprivation does not always produce maladjustment.

Conversely, some children break down under emotional stresses which most children take in their stride. Visiting a school, I was asked to investigate the case of a nine-year-old boy who was causing much concern by his highly emotional hostility. He had eight elder brothers, of whom all had been well-adjusted in school and worked in regular jobs. The mother told me that she suffered from depressed moods, during which she threatened to desert the family. The boy admitted that this used to worry him, but when I asked him what his elder brothers thought about it, he replied, "They say she won't." They were emotionally robust enough to brush off her threats as "just talk" when their mother was fed up.

These apparent exceptions to the general effects of deprivation have made students of child behavior aware that there must be some factor of individual vulnerability that determines to what extent a child reacts by maladjustment to anxiety creating experiences.

A clue to the nature of this vulnerability is provided by the greater liability of maladjusted children to other kinds of impairment. In the Canadian study of a large random sample of school age children referred to earlier in this book,[2] all types of maladjustment were associated with a greater than average incidence of ill health and physical maldevelopment. It was greatest—amounting to nearly twice the average incidence— in association with Depression, but this would have been partly due to the enervation caused by chronic illnesses. It was over one and a half times as high in association with Hostility and Withdrawal, 36 percent above average with Unforthcomingness, and 33 percent with Inconsequence. The ill health and physical maldevelopment were ongoing conditions, nearly all of which would have been constitutional. The only feasible explanation of their association with the basic forms of maladjustment is that the same congenital factors tended to affect both physical health and behavior. In some cases, this is seen as a vulnerability extending over several areas, producing a syndrome of multiple impairment.

Paralleling their greater liability to nearly all physical illnesses and defects, boys are more prone than girls to maladjustment. In the previously mentioned study, the only type to which this did not apply was Unforthcomingness, which was 42 percent more prevalent among girls. Withdrawal was nearly twice as prevalent among boys and Depression was over twice as common; Hostility was 29 percent more common among boys, and In consequence no less than 2½ times more so. Over all, about twice as many boys as girls were found to be maladjusted. This large sex difference is often explained by differences in the ways boys and girls are brought up, the assumption being that a certain amount of unruliness is allowed in boys, while girls are expected to be "ladylike." The weakness of this explanation is that the kinds of misbehavior defined as maladjustment could by no means be overlooked or encouraged by parents. No one would suggest that parents would condone their sons' stealing, or that normal parents would bring up their sons to be depressed or withdrawn, which—as has been seen—show the same degree of excess in boys as acting out behavior. There are, therefore, good reasons for supposing that these sex differences in adjustment are inborn. If this is so, it provides further evidence that vulnerability to maladjustment is a matter of the child's constitutional make up.

In everyday life, vulnerable children are hypersensitive to stress, react with great anxiety to insecurity, or find it difficult to control their impulses. Not all such children actually become maladjusted. Some deprivation or other conducive environment is usually needed to trigger their weakness.

VULNERABILITY AND
SOCIAL DISADVANTAGE

Variations in the prevalence of maladjustment in different types of localities give us one clue to the reasons for these variations in individual vulnerability. At a seminar which I attended a few years ago, a School Welfare Officer boasted that in the small town in England, where he worked there had not been a single case of juvenile delinquency for six years. There is indeed much less maladjustment and delinquency in small town and country districts. In the previously mentioned Canadian survey,[2] rural children were found to be better adjusted than children who attended schools serving the best areas of the city; this was consistently the case both for boys and for girls—and for overreacting and underreacting types of maladjustment. Rutter[3] was surprised to find that London children were much more maladjusted than those living on the Isle of Wight. The evidence seems to show, in short, that vulnerability to maladjustment has something to do with living in large urban areas.

Further clues are provided by the greater prevalence of behavior disturbance, poor health, and physical defects among the poorer section of the population. The British National Child Development Study[4] found that among children whose fathers were manual workers there were proportionately nearly twice as many maladjusted as among those whose fathers had non-manual occupations. The excess was spread over all types of maladjustment, including Unforthcomingness, so that it could not have been due merely to a greater amount of undisciplined behavior among working-class children. Despite the greater prevalence of maladjustment among them, the majority of working-class children are well-adjusted, and they were so even when their housing and nutrition were less adequate than they are now. Moreover, some middle- and upper-class children are maladjusted. Consequently, maladjustment is not a direct effect either of inferior living conditions or of working-class methods of child rearing or attitudes to life. We have to seek causes which are more likely to exist in association with working-class conditions, but which are not confined to them.

The greater prevalence of all kinds of behavior disturbance among the poorer sections of society is paralleled by a similar greater prevalence among them of infant mortality and congenital conditions which imply later handicap. In the Perinatal Survey,[5] infant mortality was reported as being 85 percent higher in the Registrar-General's Social Class V (unskilled manual workers) than in Social Class I (professional and managerial). Prematurity[1] as measured by the length of the pregnancy—was 55 percent more frequent in Class V than in Class I and—as measured by birth weight—over twice as prevalent in the lowest social class. Prematurity is strongly associated with subsequent childhood ill health and other handicaps, including maladjustment.[6] It, therefore, appears probable that the same conditions which cause infant mortality and child handicap can also cause a variety of behavior disturbances. Infant mortality and prematurity, by their nature, originate in events and conditions occurring at or before birth, which means that they are congenital. We are, therefore, led to ask what it is in working-class life that produces a greater likelihood of congenital damage, including vulnerability to all kinds of behavior disturbance.

PRENATAL LINKS BETWEEN HANDICAP
AND SOCIAL DISADVANTAGE

A follow up study from birth—including the pregnancies—of a representative sample of children in the West of Scotland,[7] suggests what the nature of these noxious congenital factors may be. By far the most damaging was the mother's unhappiness during the pregnancy due to severe and ongoing personal tensions. The children of these unhappy mothers suffered nearly twice the amount of handicap—both physical and behavioral—as the rest of the sample. Of these bad personal relationships, the most damaging was marital discord. A second study, covering 1300 Canadian children,[8] confirmed this finding: marital discord during the pregnancy produced a 94 percent greater than normal rate of handicap in the children. In both studies, other personal tensions arose from quarrels with neighbors, with in-laws living in the home, and with public authorities. Since these sources of stress would be more frequent under conditions of overcrowding, unemployment, and low income, it is understandable that they would wreak more havoc in the disadvantaged sections of the community. It is of interest to note that interpersonal problems during the pregnancy, although fewer in number, had even more damaging effects on the children in the more affluent sections of the community. The tensions, not the poverty were primary. But the increased risk of personal problems that goes with poverty was responsible for the greater prevalence of congenital damage of all kinds among the poor.

These injurious influences are seen at their severest in the problem family, where all the safeguards against interpersonal stresses have broken down. The result is that each problem generation produces its crop of unstable, unhealthy, delinquent, and retarded children who, in turn, perpetuate the damaging stresses in subsequent generations. This phenomenon—the seemingly endless cycle of deprivation and handicap—has been attributed to "bad stock." But the handicaps are too varied to admit of a simple genetic explanation, and the same applies to the greater prevalence of maladjustment and other handicaps among the disadvantaged sections of the population in general. Moreover, the working classes of the advanced industrial nations have emerged too recently, in genetic terms, from rural populations for stable genetic differences between classes to have evolved.

In short, we are left with only one explanation for the disproportionate amount of handicap found in the disadvantaged sections of industrial populations: the affected children are damaged prenatally by the interpersonal tensions generated by poverty and overcrowding. This does not rule out a genetic factor. Many studies of animal populations have shown that overcrowding activates a genetic propensity to lethal defect, ill health, and behavior disturbance, all of which serve to cut down numbers to the level that eliminates the stresses of overcrowding. There is reason to believe that the same mechanisms operate in the human species.[9] The problem family does not have an accumulation of inferior genes. The potentially destructive genes are present in all of us, but they become activated only by the sorts of stresses—primarily personal tensions but also certain infectious diseases—which are the outcome of overcrowding.

When we contemplate the two bodies of evidence concerning social background and maladjustment, we find, on the one hand, that children in large urban areas are more maladjusted, and, on the other, that those born in families where there are stressful marital and neighborly relationships are more vulnerable to common handicaps, including maladjustment. If we look more closely at the contrasting modes of life in cities and in small communities we see that these two sets of findings are really only different aspects of the same sequence of causes and effects.

COMMUNITY SAFEGUARDS AGAINST
THE CONDITIONS PRODUCING MALADJUSTMENT

The fact that the city poor live in crowded conditions and have to suffer the discomfort of close proximity to neighbors is only one aspect of the social stress to which they are subjected. Harriett Wilson[10] noted that the 50 problem families she studied were isolated from relatives and had no friends. In a settled area, whether urban or rural, each woman usually has a close friend to whom she can turn for help, and from whom she can draw comfort in talking about her family problems. Also, the family is usually not far from grandparents whom they visit frequently. However, many urban neighborhoods are composed of families who have moved into them from afar, and these families are consequently separated from relatives and friends. Membership in a relatively small community composed of individuals who have seen each other grow up and will see how each others' children behave carries with it a personal accountability. Every man and woman knows that the rest of the community will be proud of them if they lead honest, regular lives and raise well-behaved children. If they meet these standards, they will be called decent people, and others will mix with them and let their children mix with their children. The younger generation is brought up to be respectful to elders and generally to maintain the family's good name. Husbands and wives are under a social pressure to accommodate themselves to each other and to adjust to their differences. Deserting the family means also deserting one's friends whom one has known from childhood. Moreover, the village family cannot "disappear" so easily as can the urban family when they get into debt or otherwise make life uncomfortable for themselves. The result is that in many urban neighborhoods largely composed of newcomers, people tend to keep to themselves. These neighborhoods are not communities; they are conglomerations of leaderless, powerless people who get on each others' nerves.

One of the differences between life in a well integrated community and life among a collection of individuals without any community accountability is in the way the children are brought up. In the close knit community, with full social accountability, the children are taught restraint ("minding their manners"). They know that they always have to consider, and face, the consequences of their behavior. In the disorganized neighborhood, the parents, having already more troubles than they can cope with, are inclined to be blind to their children's misbehavior.

Widespread maladjustment, vandalism, and delinquency provide an index of social disintegration; the families of these areas lack community ties and hence an incentive to maintain their good name. Yet even within a disadvantaged neighborhood, there are some families who maintain respectable standards within their limited means, and raise well-adjusted children. Social workers know that every street—and even each section of a street—has a reputation for being respectable or disreputable. The respectable sections consist of those families who are integrated into small communities; in the disreputable sections, the residents are on bad terms with people outside the family, avoid involvements for fear of quarreling, and move from one broken down neighborhood to another.

The social historian would be able to trace the process by which the propertyless immigrants into the cities during the Industrial Revolution have gradually become integrated into innumerable small communities. The historian would note that people became members of church and chapel congregations, the Salvation Army, innumerable local branches of trade unions, working men's clubs, closed societies, women's guilds, and educational associations.

In the case of young people, community reintegration was effected through the club movement (Scouts, Boys' Clubs, and so on). The value of these organizations was that they brought young people under the influence of responsible adults outside the family, and enabled them to make friendships among themselves that could last for life. Schools also provided a locus for a younger generation in a new community to get to know each other and to make friendships, but the memories of school which the adult members bore were such that the schools themselves, with certain exceptions, did not become centers of community life.

Unfortunately, these community organizations, of both adults and youth, seem to have lost their hold. The material effects of the resulting disorganization are seen in vandalized pay phones, bus and park shelters, and school buildings. The social effects are a high delinquency rate, poor standards of attainment in school, and the prevalence of all sorts of maladjustment.

EDUCATION THROUGH SOCIAL ACTION PROJECTS

The repair of this cultural disintegration has to be made through a process of education. The crucial issue is the form it should take. General exhortations and complaints about the decay of family life will be as ineffective as they have always been. Only the exceptional few are sensitive to such abstract appeals. The majority require a practical form of education which is linked to their own needs, and which enables them to learn from their own activity and experience.

Local community projects formed for the purpose of improving amenities and combating vandalism are examples of practical education. A good example is that at Widnes in Lancashire, England, devised and guided by Social and Community Planning Research.[11] Its focus was a public housing project whose residents had resigned themselves to the violence and vandalism of the local youth, felt no pride in living in the project, and only wanted to get out. There were also deep suspicions of the local council and its officials. By a series of consultative meetings with residents, the planners were able to initiate social activities through which people could get to know each other. When neighbors discovered a common concern about life in the project, they supported each other in improving amenities and controlling the behavior of the local youth. The result was that the physical environment was vastly improved—with fewer signs of litter, broken glass and vandalism generally. Newly planted trees survived in defiance of prediction, and people began to care for their front gardens. The police reported a dramatic decrease in crime and a calming effect on the small number of families who had been terrorizing the neighborhood.

EDUCATION IN FAMILY RELATIONSHIPS

The wider aspect of prevention through education is whether it may be possible to establish a practice of family relationships based on knowledge, rather than on blind instinct or fashions which tend to be reactions against the unhappy experiences of the previous generation. Cultural traditions are hard to change, yet they yield, sometimes violently, to necessity. The temperance and prohibition movements in the United States arose from experience of the devastating effects of alcoholism on family life. It may be that the next generation—having suffered in their childhoods from distress and hardship caused by broken homes—will insist on the importance of permanence in marriage. Each phase of dissoluteness ultimately generates a compensating puritanism.

Nevertheless, we cannot wait for these spontaneous movements of cultural reintegration to occur, especially as the reactions tend to go to extremes which, in turn, generate a compensating libertinism, such as we are now undergoing. Nor can those young people who will be the parents of the next generation be provided with direct experience of all the various faults in family life that produce maladjustment. Yet direct instruction, especially of an abstract and theoretical type, succeeds only with those few who have both an inclination to learn and good learning skills. For the majority, it still holds true that learning, to be effective and useful, has to be through activity and experience.

The reactions of stressed and frustrated parents—and of their children—to emotional abuse, are part of the behavioral repertoire of a universal human nature. These reactions are open to everyone's experience because they are happening around us to some degree all the time. We can

learn to recognize these basic instinctive reactions in their normal manifestations and to understand how, under pressure, they become "maladjusted."

A weakness of pedagogues is that they are are vocal on principles but
silent on their application. I may, therefore, be excused if I quote—as one
method of stimulating natural learning through activity and experience—
the training of my psychology students in making their own observations
about human behavior in everyday life. After being given case history illus-
trations of the reactions to be observed, they recorded occurrences, both
normal and pathological, from their own experience or, failing that, from
their reading or filmgoing. Some of these are now quoted, partly for their
own interest and partly to serve as material for similar courses.

In studying the processes of avoidance, many students immediately
recognized their tendency to put off writing difficult essays; some noted
an impulse to avoid looking when they feared an accident. A student who
smoked admitted that she avoided reading articles on the dangers of
smoking. An instance of such normal avoidance in a three-year-old girl was
her habit of closing her eyes and turning her head away, either when a
stranger addressed her or when a familiar person asked her a question to
which she did not know the answer. Plunging into some other, preferably
exciting activity as a means of forgetting—still within the limits of
normality—was exemplified by a boy who went for a fast ride on his
motorcycle whenever he was upset about something.

Another student reported how fantasies of excitement—in the form
of the planning of a perfect robbery—were used by a young man to stop
him from thinking about a girl friend who had just given him up.

My students recounted many instances of how hostility is used to
kill a love which is not returned. A girl receives a letter from her boy-
friend, to whom she considered herself almost engaged. Suddenly she yells
out, "I hate you," and, continuing to scream, lists all his faults and de-
clares she never wants to see him again. He had informed her that he did
not love her, and he proposed a discontinuance of the relationship. Some
time later, she began to go out with a friend of her former lover. Her hate
for the latter then vanished, and she was able to accept him as a friend.
The phase of hostility had fulfilled its natural function of freeing the rejected one from an unrewarding emotional bond and enabling her to make
a new attachment. This is an example of the normal operation of hostility,
which not only brings no bad consequences but serves a useful purpose.

My students provided me with other examples. A little girl nursed her sick puppy devotedly, but on hearing it had to be destroyed began to cry and said she hated it. A boy, learning that his much loved grandmother with whom he lived proposed to send him to boarding school, suddenly began to steal from her, stayed away from home, and began to associate with a shepherd—after a year at school, however, he realized that his grandmother's action was not one of rejection, and his hostility vanished.

Other examples of hostility recounted by my students illustrate a feature of our contemporary culture, namely, the extent to which unrestrained expressions of anger have become accepted as normal. A seven-year-old boy, often left alone by his parents, frequented a neighbor's house and become attached to an older boy in that family. When the neighbor family went out for the day without taking him, as he had hoped, the youngster destroyed their tulip bed. He admitted doing it, but added that he was not sorry. A woman student related how, as a girl of six, she was given a doll's house of which she became very fond. One day when she was naughty and her mother threatened to take it away and give it to someone else, she smashed it up. Here is a final example of this tradition of the free expression of hostility. A young husband went along with his wife's possessiveness by never leaving her company. One weekend, however, he decided to go hunting with a friend, although the couple would otherwise have gone together to a formal occasion that she was greatly looking forward to. While he was away, she broke all his fishing rods and reels, then packed her things and went to her mother. On his return, the husband tried to contact her, but she remained sullen and moody.

THE LEARNING OF RESTRAINT

These samplings of behavior from our contemporary way of life carry an important lesson for the prevention of maladjustment. Having become so much the norm, they cannot in themselves—at any rate in children—be regarded as maladjusted. But such lack of restraint continued into adulthood begins to have serious cultural and biological consequences. If a marital relationship is so frail that it can be broken by a single loss of temper, it bodes ill for the stability of family life. It risks denying the next generation of children the assurance of permanence without which they may react by maladjustment. And evidence has been quoted that pregnancies wracked by discord are likely to result in physically and emotionally damaged children.

Far from being seen as dangerous, free indulgence in emotion is coming to be regarded as right and proper. A fashionable, albeit primitive, psychology which conceives of emotions as having the physical properties of liquids has it that they will wreak havoc in the psyche if they are "bottled up." Many people feel they have a right to express their sentiments, however wounding they may be; they also believe that a good quarrel is somehow therapeutic. This cannot be so, because during a quarrel hurtful things are said which produce further alienation; insofar as threats of desertion are made, trust is undermined and further hostility is generated as a means of reducing the pain of the separation. Fighting marriages seldom last.

In some traditional cultures, open quarreling within the extended family is regarded as an inexcusable offense. It was once an understood thing in our own culture that adults did not quarrel in front of children. Even at the price of denying some people what they regard as their right to free expression of their emotions, these traditions of restraint need to be reinstated.

In the contemporary emphasis upon the individual's rights and freedom of action, it has often been forgotten that a delicate balance has to be maintained between rights and responsibilities—between one's own desires and the rights and welfare of others. The Me-culture saw the right of the individual to do what he or she likes as the ultimate good and social restraints as the ultimate evil. This philosophy received its most forthright expression—and was practiced to its ultimate logic—by the Marquis de Sade. When it is realized that giving free play to primitive impulses can cause not only the distress that is seen, but the physical and emotional maiming of the next generation, the balance of the individual's rights and responsibilities swings decisively toward restraint as the central virtue of a civilized humanity.

Parents who are concerned about the future happiness of their children and of their children's children may ask themselves how to strike a balance between this need for a civilized restraint and the prevailing permissiveness. Burton White, the American authority on the preschool child, contents himself with emphasizing one simple principle: in any showdown with a young child the parent's and not the child's will should prevail. The same, as regards fundamentals, applies to handling of children up to and through adolescence. This rule has, nevertheless, to be tempered by kindness and flexibility. Because of our natural human tendency to dominate, parents have continually to ask themselves: "Am I requiring this because I want to control my child's life or because it is really critical that the child be protected from his or her inexperience?" I am not going to say that a parent should reason endlessly with a child. Adolescents have inexhaustible resources of inexperience and illogic to fall back upon, and the resulting arguments can wear a parent out. Some requirements—good table manners, personal cleanliness, wearing shoes, and protecting the older generation from needless stress—are embedded in the experience and wisdom of centuries. To justify them in debate would demand a greater knowledge of cultural anthropology, animal behavior, nutrition and disease, and so on, than most parents have. This is not to say that one should not give a reason if one can, or not listen to the youngster's point of view; but the parent's considered ruling should prevail.

Many modern parents yield to what they disapprove for fear of "losing" their children. This is a groundless anxiety. The need of children for the support and affection of their parents is stronger than their need for peer attachments. There is no fundamental conflict involved. A boy or girl can enjoy the companionship of friends without getting drunk, taking drugs, or being a danger on the roads or sexually promiscuous. Further, a young person can be happy without denying the adults of the family the right to lead an orderly and peaceful life. A lesson that can be learned from the study of animal populations is that survival of the whole group depends upon the physical and emotional health of the *parent* generation. In the human, as in animal species, harassment leads ultimately to depression, irritability, vicious attacks on the young, and stress disease. The indulged child tends in the end to become such a source of stress—in some circumstances, inducing the parent to lose self-control and threaten to desert or to injure or abandon the child. In short, it is not discipline but indulgence, which presents a threat to the existence of the family and the future happiness of the children.

References

CHAPTER 1

[1] C. M. Drillien, *The Growth and Development of the Prematurely Born Infant* (Livingstone, Edinburgh: 1964).

[2] R. Lapouse, and M. A. Monk, "An epidemiologic study of behavior characteristics in children," *American Journal of Public Health 48* (1958): 1134-44.

[3] M. Cleugh, *Psychology in the Service of the School* (Methuen, London: 1951).

[4] J. Bowlby, "Forty-four juvenile thieves: their characteristics and home life, "*International Journal of Psycho-analysis 25* (1944): 1-57.

[5] E. E. Maccoby, J. J. Johnson, and R. M. Church, "Community integration and the social control of juvenile delinquency," *Journal of Social Issues 14* (1958): 38-51.

[6] D. J. West and D. P. Farrington, *Who Becomes Delinquent?* (Heinemann, London: 1973).

[7] J. J. Conger and W. C. Miller, *Personality, Social Class and Delinquency.* (New York: Wiley, 1966).

[8] D. H. Stott and N. C. Marston, *"The Bristol Social Adjustment Guides* (San Diego, Cal.: EDITS, P.O. Box 7234).

[9] C. G. Jung, *Modern Man in Search of a Soul* (London: Routledge, 1933).

CHAPTER 2

[1] J. Bowlby (1944), *see* Chap. 1.

[2] W. Goldfarb, "Infant rearing and problem behavior," *American Journal of Orthopsychiatry 13* (1943): 249.

[3] W. Goldfarb, "Effects of early institutional care on infant personality," *Journal of Experimental Education 12* (1943-4): 106-129.

[4] W. Goldfarb, "Effects of psychological deprivation in infancy and subsequent stimulation," *American Journal of Psychiatry 102* (1945-6): 18-33.

[5] R. A. Spitz, "Hospitalism," *Psycho-analytic Study of the Child 1* (1945): 53-74.

[6] S. R. Pinneau, "The infantile disorder of hospitalism and anaclitic depression," *Psychological Bulletin 52* (1955): 429-452 (and subsequent issues).

[7] J. Bowlby, M. Ainsworth, M. Boston, and D. Rosenbluth, "The effects of mother-child separation: a follow-up study," *British Journal of Medical Psychology 29* (1956): 211-247.

[8] D. H. Stott, "The effects of separation from the mother in early life," *Lanceti* (1956): 624-628.

[9] S. Naess, "Mother-child separation and delinquency," *British Journal of Delinquency 10* (1959): 22-35.

[10] H. R. Schaffer and W. M. Callender, "Psychologic effects of hospitalization in infancy," *Pediatrics 24* (1959): 528-539.

[11] H. Lewis, *Deprived Children.* (London: Nuffield Foundation and Oxford University Press, (1954).

[12] M. L. Kellmer Pringle and V. Bossio "Early, prolonged separation and

emotional maladjustment," *Journal of Child Psychology and Psychiatry 1* (1960): 37-48.

[13] M. L. Kellmer, Pringle and V. Bossio, "A study of deprived children Part I," *Vita Humana 1* (1958): 65-92.

[14] H. R. Schaffer and P. Emerson, "The development of social attachments in infancy," *Monograph of the Society for Research in Child development* 29 iii No. 94 (1964).

[15] J. Watson, *Behaviourism* (London: Kegan Paul, 1925).

CHAPTER 3

[1] D. H. Stott, *Delinquency and Human Nature* (Carnegie U.K. Trust, 1950. 2nd Edition (Baltimore: University Park Press, and Sevenoaks, Kent: Hodder and Stoughton 1980).

CHAPTER 4

[1] D. H. Stott, (1950), *see* Chap. 3.

[2] B. Bettelheim, *Love Is Not Enough* (Glencoe, Ill.: The Free Press, 1973).

[3] D. H. Stott, "A follow-up study from birth of the outcome of different prenatal stresses," *Developmental Medicine and Child Neurology 15* (1973): 770-787.

[4] D. H. Stott and S. A. Latchford "Prenatal antecedents of child health, development and behavior," *Journal of Child Psychiatry 15* (1976): 161-191.

CHAPTER 5

[1] R. C. Bealer, F. K. Willitis, and P. R. Maida, "The rebellious youth subculture—a myth." In R. E. Muuss (ed.) *Adolescent Behavior and Society: A Book of Readings.* (New York: Random House, 1971).

[2] J. C. Latina and J. L. Schembera "Volunteer homes for status offenders: an alternative to detention," *Federal Probation 40* (1976): 45-49.

[3] W. McCord and J. McCord, *Origins of Crime* (New York: Columbia University Press, 1959).

[4] D. H. Stott (1950), *see* Chap. 3.

CHAPTER 6

[1] D. H. Stott, Delinquency: The Problem and its Prevention. pp. 169-175. (Jamaica, New York. SP Medical and Scientific Publications 1982).
[2] ——— (1950) see Chap. 3.

CHAPTER 7

[1] J. Adamson, *Living Free* (Glasgow: Collins, Fontana Books, 1961).
[2] C. Hutt and R. Bhavnani, "Predictions from play." In J. S. Bruner, A. Jolly and K. Sylva (eds.) *Play: Its Role in Development and Evolution.* (Harmondsworth, Middlesex: Penguin Books, 1976).
[3] R. W. White, "Motivation reconsidered: the concept of competence," *Psychological Review 66* (1959): 297-333.
[4] D. H. Stott, "An empirical approach to motivation based on the behaviour of a young child," *Journal of Child Psychology and Psychiatry 2* (1961): 97-117.
[5] L. B. Murphy, *The Widening World of Childhood* (Chicago: Basic Books, 1962).
[6] D. H. Stott, *Programmed Reading Kit* (Edinburgh: Holmes McDougall, 1962).
[7] D. H. Stott, *Flying Start Learning to Learn Kit* (Chicago and Toronto: Science Research Associates, 1971).
[8] D. H. Stott, "Evidence for a congenital factor in maladjustment and delinquency," *American Journal of Psychiatry 118* (1962): 781-794.
[9] D. H. Stott, N. C. Marston, and S. J. Neill, *Taxonomy of Behavior Disturbance* Guelph: Brook Educational Publishing, Box 1171 (1975).
[10] D. H. Stott, (1973), see Chap 4.
[11] D. H. Stott, and S. A. Latchford (1976), see Chap 4.
[12] D. H. Stott, "Evidence for prenatal impairment of temperament in mentally handicapped children," *Vita Humana 4* (1959): 57-76.
[13] D. H. Stott, "Pseudo-retardation as a form of learning disability: the case of Jean," *Journal of Learning Disabilities 9* (1976): 354-364.
[14] D. H. Stott, "Jean: a case of pseudo-retardation." In M. F. Freehill (ed.), *Disturbed and Troubled Children* (New York: Spectrum, 1973).
[15] D. H. Stott, and J. D. Sharp, *Effectiveness Motivation Scale.* (Windsor: National Foundation for Educational Research, 1976).

CHAPTER 8

[1] M. O'Neill, in D. H. Stott, *The Hard-to-Teach Child*. University Park Press, Baltimore.

[2] D. H. Stott (1971), *see* Chap 7.

[3] "Learning to Learn," film produced by Audio-Visual Dept., University of Guelph, Guelph, Ontario.

[4] D. H. Stott, N. C. Marston and S. J. Neill (1975), *see* Chap 7.

[5] D. J. Safer and R. P. Allen, *Hyperactive Children* (Baltimore: University Park Press, 1976).

[6] A. O. Ross, *Psychological Aspects of Learning Disabilities and Reading Disorders* (New York: McGraw-Hill, 1976).

[7] J. S. Bruner, A. Jolly, and K. Sylva, *Play: Its Role in Development and Evolution* (Harmondsworth: Penquin Books, 1976).

[8] D. H. Stott, (1971), *see* Chap 7.

[9] M. Wignall, (1971) "Say and Do Rhymes." In *Manual to Flying Start Kit,* as reference 8.

[10] S. Walker, "Drugging the American child: we've been too cavalier about hyperactivity," *Journal of Learning Disabilities 6* (1975): 354-358.

[11] B. Feingold, *Why your Child is Hyperactive* (New York: Random House, 1975).

[12] W. G. Crook, "Can what a child eats make him dull, stupid, or hyperactive?" *Journal of Learning Disabilities 13* (1980): 281-286.

[13] L. Kohlberg, "Moral education in the schools: a developmental view." In R. E. Muuss (ed.), *Adolescent Behavior and Society: A Book of Readings* (New York: Random House, 1971).

[14] D. H. Stott, (1950), *see* Chap 3.

CHAPTER 9

[1] H. Lewis (1954), *see* Chap. 2.

[2] D. H. Stott, N. C. Marston, and S. J. Neill (1975), *see* Chap 7.

[3] M. Rutter "Why are London children so disturbed?" *Proceedings of the Royal Society of Medicine 66* (1973): 1221-1225.

[4] R. Davie, N. R. Butler, and N. Goldstein, *From Birth to Seven: Second Report of the National Child Development Study* (London: Longman and National Children's Bureau, 1972).

[5] N. R. Butler and D. F. Bonham, *Perinatal Mortality: First Report of the British Perinatal Mortality Survey* (Edinburgh: Livingstone, 1963).

[6] C. M. Drillien (1964), *see* Chap 1.

[7] D. H. Stott (1973), *see* Chap 4.

[8] D. H. Stott and S. A. Latchford (1976), *see* Chap 4.

[9] D. H. Stott "Cultural and natural checks on population growth." in M. F. A. Montagu (ed.), *Culture and the Evolution of Man* (New York: Oxford University Press, 1962). And in A. P. Vayda (ed.), *Environmental and Cultural Behavior* (New York: American Museum Source Books in Anthropology, The Natural History Press, 1962).

[10] H. Wilson, *Delinquency and Child Neglect* (London: Allen & Unwin, 1962).

[11] National Association for the Care and Resettlement of Offenders, and Social and Community Planning Research (c. 1977), *Vandalism: An Approach Through Consultation, and Other Reports.*

Short list of recommended reading

Love is Not Enough, by Bruno Bettelheim. Free Press, Glencoe, Illinois, 1973.

Disturbed and Troubled Children, edited by Maurice F. Freehill. Spectrum Publications, New York, 1973.

The Emotionally Disturbed Child in the Classroom, by Frank M. Hewett. Allyn and Bacon Inc., Boston, Mass., 1968.

The Widening World of Childhood, by Lois B. Murphy. Basic Books, Chicago, 1962.

Delinquency and Human Nature, by Denis H. Stott. Hodder and Stooughton, Sevenoaks, Kent; University Park Press, Baltimore, Maryland. Second Edition, 1980.

The Hard-to-Teach Child, by Denis H. Stott. University Park Press, Baltimore, Maryland. 1978.

Delinquency: The Problem and its Prevention, by Denis H. Stott. SP Medical and Scientific Publications, Jamaica, New York, 1982.

Index

Handicaps *(continued)*
  and social disadvantage, 120
  of temperament, 49, 82, 94-114,
    106, 111
heart disease, 108
high effectiveness, 99, 102
hospitalization, 17, 19, 21, 22, 61
hostels, 39, 43
hostility, 6, 8, 9, 20, 21, 24, 30, 37, 42,
    45, 51, 53-55, 58-9, 64-8,
    70, 73, 92, 94, 110, 112, 116,
    124-5
  treatment of, 65
Hutt, C., 78, 95, 131
hyperactivity, 94-114, 105

illegitimacy, 26, 47
illness:
  childhood, 72, 116
  psychosomatic, 127
impairment:
  collateral, 98, 116
  mental, 59
  neural, 62
imprinting, in animals, 15
improvability, 101
inattentiveness, 100
inconsequence, 92, 112, 116
  congenital, 97
  high-effectiveness, 95-6, 100, 101
  motor-impaired, 97
  neurally impaired, 96, 98
  treatment of, 101
independence, 49
individual rights, 126
indulgence, 127
Industrial Revolution, 121
infant mortality, 118
infectious diseases, 120
inferiority, feelings of, 12, 32, 64
inhibitions:
  affectional, 27
  failure of, 100, 108
inhibitory mechanisms, 100

injury, 7
instinctive behavior, 11, 47, 50, 70, 93,
    123
institutionalization, 20, 23, 29, 41, 63,
    92, 115
intelligence, 21, 85
interviewing parents, 69-70, 72-76
IQ, 82, 89, 96
irritable-depressive intolerance, 70-71
irritability, 127

jealousy, 13, 64
Jolly A., 132
Jung, C.G., 13

Kingswood Training School, 42
Klein, Melanie, 15
Kohlberg L., 132

labeling, 6
lack of concern, normal, 112
Lapouse, R., 128
Latina, J.C., 130
learning, 82, 104
  games, 81, 101, 102, 103, 106
  style, 86
  difficulties, 95, 98
Learning to Learn Film, 96, 101
Lewis, Hilda, 22, 115, 129, 132
libertinism, 123
literacy, 87
localties:
  disadvantaged, 9
  working-class, 10
Lorenz C., 15
loyalty-testing, 21, 34, 75
lying, 48

Maccoby, Eleanor E., 9, 128
magistrates, 7
Maida, P.R., 130